HELD NOT HAUNTED

Darkness to Deliverance

Delphia Leffew

Published by Delphia Leffew Publishing
ISBN: 979-8-9948128-0-8
Paperback edition
Printed in the United States of America.

Author's Note

For years, I chose silence. I believed it was strength. God has called me out of it because my testimony is where my faith was forged.

This book is my obedience.

I've carried grief, shame, spiritual battles, and the weight of my own choices. Every chapter in this book is surrender. Every word is proof that God can redeem what we hide, fear, and what we think is too broken to be used.

Held Not Haunted: Darkness to Deliverance isn't a story of perfection. It's a story of grace. If God can do this for me, nothing is beyond His reach for others.

I lived unsure of who I was. I didn't yet understand that I was formed with intention, called with purpose, and loved without condition. Without that knowledge, I mistook fear and insecurity for truth.

***"My people are destroyed for lack of knowledge."* (Hosea 4:6)**

That was me. Grace and mercy interrupted my ignorance. When I finally stopped striving and allowed myself to break, I discovered something steady beneath it all—I had been held the whole time.

Lord, You waste nothing. Take my story and use it in ways only You can. Let what has been pain for me become hope, healing, and freedom for someone else. And let it all be for Your glory.

Acknowledgments

First and foremost, I give honor and praise to God. What He has restored, healed, and redeemed in my life is nothing short of grace and mercy. Jesus Christ has been my refuge, my steady anchor through every season of this journey. This book exists because He carried me when I could not carry myself.

To my husband, thank you for walking with me through the seasons of growth and surrender. Your faith and steady support have mattered more than I can put into words.

To my mother-in-law, thank you for your prayers and for the example of a life rooted in Christ. Your consistency and quiet strength have had a significant influence in my walk with God.

I am deeply grateful for my church, Christ Family Church. It was there that truth became personal, surrender became real, and healing finally began. Thank you to my pastors for faithful leadership and unwavering dedication to Scripture.

A Seed

Some children grow up in homes where faith is part of the air they breathe—where prayers are spoken over dinner tables and Bibles sit open on coffee tables. That was not the home I was born into.

Two kids—twenty and seventeen—were navigating adulthood and marriage when they were faced with the responsibility of parenthood. Life had barely begun for them, yet the weight of raising a child was placed in their hands. In October 1980, that young couple welcomed me into the world. I would be their only daughter—the oldest of three children, stair-stepped in age.

When children come this early in life, most parents are not prepared mentally, spiritually, or financially. All too often, wisdom, stability, and direction are still developing for most. As an adult now, I can see how young and inexperienced they truly were.

Our home did not feel like a holy environment. It lacked the quiet peace that settles over a house when Christ is the center of it. There was no spiritual covering, no godly foundation beneath our feet, and no sense of the security that comes when a home is anchored in faith.

Growing up, God and Jesus were names I don't remember hearing spoken in our home. There were no bedtime prayers, no Bible stories at the kitchen table, and no conversations about faith guiding our days.

When I was seven years old, an elderly family friend—my babysitter's mother, Lois—would introduce me to them. Lois was gentle and patient, the kind of woman whose presence felt safe. Something inside of me responded when she spoke about God. I didn't have the words to explain it then, but I felt a pull deep in my heart. A spark. A curiosity about something holy that I wanted to understand.

I remember eagerly getting ready early on a few Sunday mornings. No one had to wake me or remind me to go. I would dress myself, putting on one of the few outfits I thought might be close to church-worthy, and was out of the door.

From our house, I would walk a narrow path through the woods until I reached an old abandoned church. There I would wait for Lois to come by and pick me up. I was only seven years old, there by the roadside with the quiet of the morning surrounding me, eagerly waiting.

It amazes me now to think that a little girl who was afraid still walked the wooded trail alone, just to get to go to church. But even then, something inside me knew I needed to be there. Something in my heart was stirring toward God long before I fully understood who He was.

That church welcomed me with open arms—a little girl who, I am sure, sometimes looked like she might have just rolled right out of bed. Who knows if my hair was even brushed or fixed properly. But I showed up.

Somehow, being there felt steady. A place where I belonged, even before I understood why. Inside that small white church, I still remember standing in the choir. In my hands a red songbook that I would flip through quickly to bellow out the words on the page so boldly. Many years later I would learn *that book* was called a red-back hymnal, but at the time it was simply *the book* everyone used.

Someone even gave me a tambourine that was just for me. My name was even written on it. I can still remember the sound of those little metal jingles ringing through the music as I shook it with all the enthusiasm a seven-year-old could muster.

For the first time, I had a place in the house of the Lord. I wasn't just watching from the sidelines—I was part of it. I was seeking without fear. A spark had begun to smolder inside me, quietly and steadily. But that spark never had the chance to fully ignite. While something holy was beginning to stir in my heart, another atmosphere waited at home. As a child, I often felt a heaviness there—sometimes quiet, sometimes erupting, but always present.

Responsibility was not something I would slowly grow into. It was something that seemed to be placed on my shoulders early. Alongside responsibility, I also carried guilt. By seven years old, I had already seen things I should have never had to witness that I carried in silence. Moments that were far too heavy for a young heart to understand. The weight of those experiences settled deep inside me. It created a guilt that was never mine to carry, yet somehow it wrapped itself around my heart as though it was.

While a small spark of faith was beginning to flicker inside me, something else had already begun planting its own seeds. And seeds—whether holy or harmful—never stay buried forever.

Eventually, holding the silence and guilt would consume me. In my innocence, I finally broke the quiet asking, *"Why don't you get divorced?"* I didn't say it to cause trouble. I didn't say it out of anger. I said it because my heart couldn't hold what it had been absorbing any longer.

When the divorce finally came, I felt relief—but also a new layer of guilt. Relief because I no longer had to carry what I thought was secret. What I had assumed had been hidden inside our home was now fully exposed and openly discussed, not only within our walls but beyond them. Family members and friends were openly discussing our lives, and children were listening. I'll admit there was a measure of personal freedom in that exposure. But a new guilt settled in, as if I had somehow set everything into motion.

It was 1988. It would take years before I would realize we were an anomaly. Children rarely lived with their father back then. Being the only female in our divorced home brought a new sense of responsibility in my mind. I shifted from a sister to a parent. I took my newly self-assigned role seriously. And boy, did I ever. I felt like I had a gap to fill.

Like all divorces, there is transition to a new norm. I wish I could say things were better. My middle brother struggled through the change. This would be felt and managed by all for years to come. My baby brother, only three at the time, needed care. While I felt responsible for both, Nathan—the youngest—would forever feel more like my child than my brother. I stepped into a mothering role long before I ever understood what motherhood was. But I had a purpose…*I was needed.*

The divorce was a pivotal point for our family. I celebrated it. However, it brought changes my little mind could not foresee. I had believed this change would bring newfound peace, but instead for me it felt like a new door of instability and confusion.

I had already established an unsteady understanding of family and love. I can't remember hearing "I love you" spoken often if at all, or experiencing the kind of affection and tenderness a child really needs. There would be more that would come that deepened the fractures already formed in my heart.

The enemy was quietly planting something else through these changes: the belief that I had to be strong. There was no opportunity for weakness. I was only eight by this point and I was already trying to protect myself from hurt. I felt the need to try to carry the weight of my brothers, my home, and my world. I held the responsibility of protecting others.

I was far too young to understand it then, but that divorce—along with the adults surrounding me—the enemy would use to forge a lie that would shape decades of my life:

"You are alone."

With every divorce, there is a before and an after, marked by the changes it brings. In my case, church had disappeared long before the divorce was final. That meant God was no longer on my radar. However, a seed had been planted thanks to that elderly family friend. When God plants a seed, hell cannot destroy it.

Home

A couple of years after my parents' divorce, I moved into my grandparents' home. "Home" would become their singlewide trailer with an addition built on to the front. Our backyard wasn't a yard at all. There was no grass—just a gravel circle drive scattered with my grandfather's excavating equipment, piles of rock, occasionally dirt, years of collected odds and ends—most would agree was junk. It was far from pretty by any standard. I would later become embarrassed of my home as I grew older because of the appearance. But this was home.

It didn't instantly become home on a set day. It quietly occurred throughout my fourth-grade year and the summer after. During this time, I was struggling with an ulcer. A child with an ulcer speaks its own story. That alone tells of the weight I was silently carrying. I had learned to swallow my feelings.

I was far from feminine or dainty. Having grown up surrounded by boys, they were my tribe. In my environment, there was no room for the conversations every young girl eventually has to face. I was reaching the age when every girl desperately needs a woman's presence and influence. I would need those awkward conversations about changing bodies and the forthcoming questions—the kind of conversations that make everyone uncomfortable, especially fathers.

I feel absolutely confident in saying no man wakes up hoping to discuss puberty with his daughter. Mine was navigating a house full of boys. He knew how to coach on the field and call plays. Teaching a daughter about training bras and puberty—I doubt he felt equipped—

and certainly not eager—to tackle those topics. There was also an expectation that moving in would help my grandmother, who had physical limitations.

Becoming Invisible

My grandparents' home wasn't chaotic in the same way my parents' had felt, but it carried its own challenges—challenges that would leave deep scars I wouldn't understand until much later.

My grandfather's skin had been baked from years of outdoor work. However, the most noticeable feature was his mammoth-sized hands. Hands you did not want reaching for you.

He was a hard man. His demeanor was cold. His words cut deep, and his tone carried an authority that didn't nurture—it silenced.

In that house, the easiest thing to be was quiet. Unseen. Small. The sound of a voice could trigger anger. My presence could quickly become an inconvenience. Blending into the background was the best way to avoid conflict or his object of annoyance.

During the ten years I lived with them, my grandfather only referred to me as *"that girl."*

Not Delphia. Never by name—just— *"that girl."*

Strangely enough, my great-grandmother—his mother-in-law—and I share the same name. Whether he truly couldn't remember it or simply chose not to use it is anyone's guess.

There is something about not being called by your name that settles in a child. It makes you feel temporary. Invisible. No one corrected him, and I never expected anyone to. I learned some things were best left alone.

I was conditioned to shrink myself. To stay quiet. To be invisible. That was my grandmother's spoken motto, which she embedded into me. It had been her survival strategy, learned throughout her years in that environment—a marriage that carried both verbal and physical scars. She passed her survival tool down to me.

My grandfather's anger ignited quickly, his irritation simmered just beneath the surface, and his words were without restraint. My goal was always the same: never present an opportunity to become the target. I *wanted* to be invisible.

My grandfather carried his own brokenness and damage. His comments were never positive toward anyone. He did not attempt to hide them either. His words were loud, deliberate, and edged in a way that ensured they landed.

He also carried a bitter jealousy toward almost everyone, both within our family and beyond. It would surface frequently. I knew what was coming every time my other grandparents would offer to take me to dinner. I would eagerly watch for their car to turn in and try to slip out the door before his comments could begin.

There were always snide remarks—something about their Cadillac, or something about a showy appearance. He also never missed an opportunity to tell me that my other grandfather had apparently once been a preacher and stepped away long before I had even been born— as if that somehow disqualified him.

I was a pre-adolescent—I didn't even know what *hypocrite* meant, but I understood its weight. I understood the tone, the condescension, the subtle superiority behind the term.

With time came clarity, the Cadillac grandparents were simply two people offering love and kindness to a child. I don't remember them ever raising their voices. They carried a peaceful quiet—so unlike the sharp edges of my hardened grandfather.

My hardened grandfather was quick with judgment and never showed gratitude. Even their generosity toward me became something to critique. He found fault in everything. Criticism was his natural element. The pattern never shifted. It was predictable.

The brokenness my grandfather carried spilled out in words, and those words carved their own damage into me. As an adult, even now I can hear a shift in tone—an edge of aggravation or anger—and I am instantly that little girl again. I want to fold inward, shrink, and retreat.

Hearing the accusations and judgment he carried toward someone who had once stood publicly in faith planted something inside me—a quiet fear that would follow me for years. Watching someone be spoken about with such contempt for stepping away from ministry left an impression. Over time, I developed an embedded scar that drove me into silence about my own faith for decades.

Careless

There were other adults who should have offered kindness—who should have offered safety, gentleness, and love—but they apparently carried their own demons. Instead of covering me and showing goodness, they projected their brokenness onto me. They cashed in on opportunities to be mean, to say cutting things, to throw shade, and to make fun of me as if my feelings were disposable.

It seemed easy for them to shame a child for the sins of her parents. Their words weren't just careless; they were intentional. They were meant to remind me of where I came from, as if my lineage determined my worth.

Their words didn't just sting; they shaped the way I saw myself. Every stab at my expense, every sarcastic comment, every moment of belittling carved another line into my spirit. I learned early that some adults used their authority not to nurture, but to wound.

I was a child, so I absorbed it all.

I didn't understand then that their cruelty had nothing to do with me and everything to do with their own unhealed places. I only knew how it made me feel: embarrassed and humiliated.

This only deepened my desire to shrink, to stay quiet, and to anticipate rejection before it arrived. It trained me to brace myself for impact in moments that should have been safe.

These wounds didn't come from strangers. They came from people who should have known better—people who should have focused on protecting a child rather than being bullies, people who should have spoken life but instead spoke poison.

Those early wounds didn't destroy me, but they did shape the way I would navigate the world for most of my life.

They became part of the battlefield used to twist my identity, to silence my voice, and to make me believe I was unworthy of love or gentleness.

This would not be the final word, nor the truth of who I was.

In my forties, the love of my Savior would heal my heart and bring freedom to those wounds. I not only forgave those who hurt me, but I also began to pray for their healing. I now understand hurt people, hurt people.

Wounds

My wounds did not appear out of nowhere. They were shaped by moments—small, sharp, unforgettable moments—that taught me to expect rejection and absence. I learned early to brace myself. Not to get too attached. Not to expect consistency. Not to believe I was worthy.

I had too many experiences that confirmed it. I was kept close for what I provided—support, or only when it benefited others—but not for who I was. Every disappointment carved another layer deeper. My hope had been deferred more times than I could count. There were birthdays when no one showed up, and phone calls that never came—promises made but broken with familiar predictability.

Every absence taught me something. Every moment of being disregarded reinforced a belief:

You are not a priority. You are forgettable.

I carried those beliefs as if they were truth.

Over time, those wounds settled deep beneath the surface of my heart. I see it clearly now—a battle had been forming inside me.

Yes, it was emotional, but it went deeper than feelings.

Somewhere along the way, I began to believe that I only mattered if I was useful. If I could help someone, fix something, or carry a burden, then maybe I had value. But without bringing something to others, I felt unworthy—disposable even.

The enemy relentlessly attacked my heart with abandonment and disappointment. He stole my sense of security. He twisted my understanding of love. Little by little, he tried to define my worth.

"There is no fear in love, but perfect love casts out fear..." (1 John 4:18) But fear had become familiar to me. I questioned where my value came from. I feared being unwanted and carried a quiet, unsettled sense that I didn't truly belong.

"Though my father and mother forsake me, the Lord will receive me." (Psalm 27:10) At the time, I didn't know He was there.

Rejection became the lens through which I saw everything. It shaped my expectations, colored my relationships, and influenced how I interpreted silence. If the enemy could convince me I was unloved, I would never believe God's love was meant for me. God's Word reminds us in Romans 8:38–39 that nothing can separate us from the love of God.

The enemy convinced me I had been abandoned. What he didn't expect was that there would be a day I would turn to the One who had never left me as was promised in Hebrews 13:5 "I will never leave you nor forsake you."

I encountered intimidating darkness, but the loneliness was the hardest part. For a long time, rejection felt like the truest thing about me.

For most of my life, I did not recognize that these deep wounds were shaping how I saw myself—the belief that I was not, and would never be, enough. The overarching fear of being unwanted, rejected, and overlooked was real. Those wounds—unspoken and unhealed— became the doorway the enemy would walk through again and again.

A few decades later, with years of repeated heartache, God would meet me in these very places where I had been struck. It would take surrender. It would take full submission to His will. But when I finally laid it all at His feet, the bondage I had carried for so long was replaced with a love I had never known.

"Whom the Son sets free is free indeed." (John 8:36)

Freedom would no longer be a concept. It would finally become my reality.

Distrust

The enemy was adamant to make me distrust people, hoping I would also distrust God. Every broken promise, every adult who didn't show up, every moment I felt ignored or forgotten—they weren't just painful; they became lessons. Lessons that taught me to expect disappointment and keep my guard up. Lessons that continued to whisper, *"You're on your own."*

If he could push me into that lonely, abandoned mindset, he was winning—and in my case, he was for a very long time. He didn't need to destroy me outright. He only needed to turn me inward and convince me I could rely only on myself.

He drove me into fierce independence. I learned to take care of myself because too often no one else did. Showing emotion felt like weakness, so I hid my feelings. Self-reliance became survival. Strength became my armor, and I wore it proudly.

Distrust and confusion were planted early. When they take root in childhood, they quietly distance you from God long before you realize what's been lost. One moment I was being introduced to Jesus by a kind family friend—standing in a choir, feeling a spark of joy rising. The next, that spark was buried beneath a new mindset being built— quiet, withdrawn, careful.

Looking back, it was strategic. Not loud. Not dramatic. Just enough disruption to create distance. Disruption was all the enemy needed.

Lack of trust and loneliness were my companions. My bedroom was the only place where peace felt guaranteed, so I often retreated there. Solitude became my shelter long before I understood its cost. That loneliness didn't stay in childhood—it followed me into friendships, relationships, adulthood, and even into the church.

Without realizing it, I built walls. I stayed guarded—always watching, always calculating how close was too close. What many interpreted as arrogance was often insecurity displayed as silence. I could be surrounded by people and still feel completely alone. My body was present, but my heart stayed tucked behind invisible barricades.

I became an expert at scanning for exits—a quick escape route, a corner where I could disappear, any way to avoid interaction. Connection felt foreign. Belonging felt impossible. I didn't understand then that I wasn't avoiding people—I was avoiding the possibility of being hurt.

Loneliness wasn't just a feeling; it became a survival strategy.

"Turn to me and be gracious to me, for I am lonely and afflicted." (Psalm 25:16) Had I known that verse then, it would have been the cry of my heart.

Even in that isolation, God saw me. He saw the walls, the fear, and the longing to belong that I had buried. In time, He would begin dismantling everything that had wrapped itself around my life like a second skin.

Doorway

The emotional atmosphere in our home was heavy, and the spiritual atmosphere was just as thick. A vulnerable little girl surrounded by instability and emotional cracks was the perfect breeding ground for confusion.

I had a total lack of understanding that spiritual hunger can easily turn into spiritual danger. By the time I was eleven, I had been exposed to things that were spiritual but not holy. Things that stirred curiosity. Things that promised control when everything around me felt out of control. Things that whispered answers when God felt distant and silent. Things that felt like access to something powerful—even if that power didn't come from God.

In my world, that doorway came through someone I loved deeply—my grandmother.

She was barely five feet tall and fragile. Her hands and feet told the truth her mouth never did. Rheumatoid arthritis had severely twisted and reshaped them into something many could only stare at. You didn't have to ask if she hurt. You could see it.

She had battled this disease since she was twenty-five years old—not for a season, not for a chapter, but for a lifetime. Always in tennis shoes. Without them, not even a single step would have been possible. Her feet had been damaged and misshapen by the disease almost as badly as her hands had been. Most people in her condition lose the ability to walk. She didn't. She refused to give up.

Her hands were deformed and aching, yet she still cooked, reached, and handled her own care. She had learned adaptations that allowed her to do what her body could no longer do. Elastic clothing replaced anything that required fastening, and specific cups sat in the cabinet because those were the only ones she could hold. These weren't dramatic changes—just quiet accommodations woven into her daily life.

She never announced her suffering. Never drew attention to it. She just suffered in silence. Just endurance. Just survival. Just getting up to do it again the next day.

A mother of four boys, her door was always open to anyone in need. She showed up whenever there was a need. It was her love language. She was never overly affectionate or one to say, "I love you," out loud, but she clearly loved deeply.

When my world felt unstable, she became my rock—the one I clung to. To me, she was my grandmother. Familiar. Safe. But also fascinating, with insights into this other world.

Sensitive

My grandmother had explored her own sensitivity—her curiosity
reaching into places that felt mysterious and powerful. Card readings.
Dream interpretations. Astrology. Intuition. Crystals and candles
offered as protection.

I was already sensitive. I sensed things I couldn't explain. I felt
things I didn't understand. I noticed what most people seemed to miss.
I was hungry to understand what I was experiencing, but I was
oblivious to the difference between spiritual sensitivity and spiritual
danger. Curiosity felt innocent. It even felt like growth.

Deception rarely introduces itself as danger. There was *some kind of*
spiritual access that could come from many sources. That knowledge
alone felt like it could elevate me. It didn't feel dark. It felt illuminating.

What should have been a hunger for God became a desire for
understanding. I wanted answers. I wanted clarity. I wanted to
understand how the spiritual realm worked.

I was too young to know that what felt harmless could become a
hook. When you are young and hungry to understand what you are
feeling, you don't know to question the source. You absorb whatever
knowledge is available. You explore conversations about "feelings,"
"signs," and "warnings."

What began as fascination slowly blurred into something else.

Curiosity and the pursuit of knowledge had opened a door. The
enemy was happily waiting on the other side.

Witchcraft did not enter my life through rituals, spells, or
cauldrons. It entered through curiosity and exposure. In our home,

confined to my grandmother's office, spiritual practices were not hidden; they were normal. Not dramatic. Not theatrical. Just part of daily life. There was no obvious indication of darkness.

This insight wasn't labeled witchcraft in our home. It was normal. My grandmother's "gift" was even referred to as a gift from God in some instances.

What appeared "white" is still dark according to God's Word. Light and dark were blurred together in ways I didn't yet know how to separate. But mixture is still mixture—even when it feels harmless.

Mixture

In our small Southern Bible Belt town, people came seeking my grandmother for help, while others kept her at arm's length. They whispered. They wondered. Some may have even feared her. She was both sought after and quietly judged. I am sure some questioned her faith altogether.

Yet I saw a softness toward God in her that few may have ever witnessed.

We visited church on a few Father's Days and Easters with my great-grandfather, her father. She went when asked because it mattered to him. She was anxious every time—not about church itself, but about the expectations— not the expectations that most would think.

She wore what she considered her Sunday best—proper dress clothes. Pressed. Respectable. But in white tennis shoes. The only shoes she could walk in. Shoes she was embarrassed by.

We would pull into the handicap parking spot, and the moment she saw the men standing at the front doors—smiling, ready with their firm handshakes—her anxiety shifted into tension. Immediately. She would take a breath, her shoulders stiffening. She knew what was coming.

By the time we reached the pew, she would glance down at her hands—already turning deep red and purple, already swelling—and shake her head with pain and frustration.

On the way home, it was the same conversation every time. Her frustration would shift to anger. Her hands were visibly crippled.

Twisted. Tender. Anyone with eyes could see it. The men never adjusted. They grabbed firmly. Squeezed hard. Pumped her hand as if it were strong and steady like everyone else's.

She carried discoloration for weeks—a painful reminder of visiting church. Why she never attempted to bypass the handshake and simply avoid pain, I will never know.

This scene repeated each visit. After two or three visits, my great-grandfather stopped asking. I'm sure he noticed the colorful physical remnants those visits had left behind.

Not once did she speak negatively about being in church. Not once did she express condemnation or conviction. Not once did she voice concern about being judged as a card reader sitting in the holy's presence. She never once framed herself as unwelcome in the house of the Lord.

Her pain wasn't from rejection. It was from expectation. The expectation to be friendly. To extend her hand when she already knew it would hurt. Her church hurt was very different from what most people experience. Her hurt was visible and physical.

This was the extent of our church involvement.

I think about that front door now. If the front door experience hadn't led to weeks of physical pain, would those visits have led to something else? Not just for her, but for me too? We will never know.

I do know she carried seeds God had planted over the course of her life. In the ten years I lived with her, occasionally I would hear her sing what had been her mother's favorite gospel song—*One Day at a Time*. It became the first gospel song etched into my heart—because of her, a card reader. Ironic when you stop and think about it. Living proof that God can use anyone—and—His seeds are indestructible.

Recently, while going through my old hope chest, I discovered an NKJV Bible she had given me, dated 1991, tucked away inside—something I had long forgotten about.

I loved that woman deeply. No doubt, she loved me. She provided for me and when everything else in my world felt unstable, she gave me a place to land.

I struggled with whether I should share the details about my grandmother publicly. The last thing I ever want to do is dishonor the memory of the woman I loved so dearly. But I also know there is power in education. Sometimes our pain—or even our ignorance—becomes the very thing God uses to help set someone else free. The greatest way I can honor her is by allowing her story to help others. I pray her story is able to do just that.

I don't condone the enemy's influence that operated in her life, but I don't judge her either. There is only one Judge. No one is without sin. "Let him who is without sin cast the first stone." I choose to live by that truth toward all humankind, not just her.

Her relationship was between her and God. That sacred space is not mine—or anyone else's—to invade. So, I leave any conversation of her salvation, her sin, and all that fell between in His hands.

I trust the goodness I witnessed in her. I hold onto the hope that one day I will see her again in Heaven. Hope exists because I know God is rich in grace and mercy toward every sinner.

Salvation is not earned by works or moral effort, but received by faith. It requires repentance—a turning of the heart—and sincere belief that Jesus Christ is Lord. When we call on His name, confess our need, and believe in His death and resurrection, we are received by grace into eternal life. Every person, while there is still breath in their lungs, has an opportunity for salvation.

Insights from my grandmother shaped the early contours of my spiritual awareness—even if neither of us understood what God was allowing at the time. I now see God would use that exposure to give me insight into a world most are oblivious to. I can now confront that world, not with fear, but with clarity and authority.

Witchcraft

I speak to educate others. I know with absolute certainty that the principalities the Bible speaks of are real.

Some people move through life convinced that witchcraft is nothing more than superstition—old stories, movie scenes, or the imagination of the overly spiritual. They laugh it off because they have never felt the strain of it, never discerned the atmosphere of it, never recognized the subtle way it surrounds us daily.
Ignorance does not make something less real. It only makes a person naive. You can't fight what you don't know exists.

Witchcraft today rarely calls itself witchcraft. It has been rebranded. What previous generations recognized as occult practice is now often presented as "New Age spirituality." It appears softer. Brighter. More empowering. It speaks the language of healing, alignment, intuition, and personal power. But at its core, it is still the pursuit of spiritual knowledge or influence apart from God.

The New Age spirit promotes ideas such as:

Manifesting your own reality

Consulting tarot or oracle cards for guidance

Astrology as identity

Crystals as protection or energy

Spirit guides

Channeling

Energy healing apart from Christ

These do not present as darkness to most. People often instead feel enlightened. That alone is why they are effective hooks.

Scripture warns clearly against "divination, mediums, sorcery, and seeking supernatural insight from any power outside of the living God." (Deuteronomy 18:10–12)

The danger is not curiosity itself. The danger is agreement with a spirit that does not originate from God. Sometimes the enemy arrives wrapped in fascination, empowerment, and "self-discovery." Not everything spiritual is holy. And not everything that feels light is from the Light.

More often, witchcraft enters through atmosphere, curiosity, and the absence of truth—through what appears harmless: horoscopes, charms, dream interpretations, even a game board like Ouija.

All too often, evil's approach is quiet, calculated, and patient. It appears in attitudes, rebellion, seduction, and confusion—the kind of darkness that does not announce itself but slowly erodes clarity and peace. In many cases, people do not even realize that what they are battling is spiritual in nature.

I didn't learn this from a sermon. This knowledge came from living through it.

Keeping silent gives darkness room to grow. It keeps confusion protected and tactics hidden. But testimony changes that. It exposes what was operating in secret. Once it is exposed, it no longer holds the same power.

Black vs White

Seeking supernatural power or knowledge from any source other than the living God is counterfeit. It is a trap designed to pull people into deception.

The witchcraft world divides itself into "good" and "bad," "white" and "black," as if darkness somehow becomes harmless when softened by renaming.

The atmosphere I was introduced to was the "white" version. Quieter, but no less spiritually charged. In my case, it looked like a deck of regular playing cards laid out for readings. Astrology and dream books within reach. Crystals meant for protection from evil. An occasional medallion tucked away for "good luck."

In the absence of God's truth, those things filled the space.

My grandmother never pushed her beliefs on me, but I was eager for understanding. She was my earliest education in what she described as spirits and their influence. She carried a deep fear of the dark demonic side of that world. She didn't speak of it often, but when she did, her reverence was unmistakable. They terrified her—and that meant they absolutely terrified me.

The Bible warns that confusion is a sign of spiritual distortion. The problem was, I wasn't consulting the Bible. I was looking anywhere and everywhere else for answers.

Simply stated—when lines blur, something is off, and it is not from God.

The lines had certainly blurred. I was trying to sort light from darkness.

There is a world beyond what is seen—a world I once believed held power. Now, as a child of God, I understand that whether it presents itself as black or white, it comes from the same source. And that source no longer holds authority. I face it without fear, knowing it must bow to the name of Jesus.

Spiritual Gift

I didn't discuss what I could only describe as spiritual experiences with anyone outside of my grandmother. She understood that world. She didn't silence me. She didn't shame me or question me. With her, I could speak freely. I could ask questions. I could breathe. There was space to explore what I didn't fully understand.

Sometimes I would see something in my mind—a picture, a moment, a warning—and later it would unfold as I had seen it. Other times, I sensed before anyone else noticed. I could feel atmospheres shift. I knew when something wasn't right.

Then there was the déjà vu. It would come suddenly—a wave of familiarity so strong it felt like time folding in on itself. It didn't feel exciting. It felt unsettling. I grew to associate these experiences with my grandmother.

This world she seemed to understand. These experiences were always celebrated as gifts. But she would pass away when I was twenty-one. My openness died with her. What once felt intriguing now felt isolating. The gift no longer— a gift. It felt like something to hide. Something that made me different.

Because of my childhood exposure, I associated anything unusual possibly tied to the spiritual realm with darkness. If it felt spiritual, I assumed it must be evil. So, I tucked it away. I feared being judged. Dismissed. Misunderstood. Or worse—labeled as something dark.

Later in life, as I spent time in God's word, I would find that scripture confirms, "Surely the Sovereign Lord does nothing without revealing His plan to His servants the prophets." (Amos 3:7) No one had prepared me or shared that God often awakens discernment before understanding follows. Spiritual sensitivity can easily turn into fear as it did in my case.

My home had not been centered around Christ. I had no framework for testing what I was experiencing. So logically, in my mind, it felt similar to the spiritual environment of my childhood, therefore it had to be evil.

The whispers were subtle:

This is just like the card readings.

This is not from God.

Without understanding of how to test the experience, anxiety followed. My chest would tighten. Fear would rush in.

What should have been discernment became dread. I had never been taught; I was supposed to test the spirit behind what I was experiencing.

Scripture says, "Beloved, do not believe every spirit, but test the spirits to see whether they are from God." (1 John 4:1) I had permission—but more importantly, a responsibility—to examine what was influencing me. Confusion twisted what should have been prophetic sensitivity into something I feared.

One of those moments I wish I had known how to test was February 2004. I had put my daughter to bed and finished my usual nighttime routine—wiping down the kitchen, picking up the house, and laying out clothes for the next day. Everything was ready.

I had been talked into doing a Pampered Chef catalog party, and the next day I was supposed to turn it in. I already had everything neatly organized, but I decided to check it one more time.

In the quiet stillness of the house, I sat down with the manila folder and went through everything again. When I finished, I set the folder beside me.

Then something strange happened.

I felt a weight and a numbness I had never experienced before. My body felt almost paralyzed. For the first time, my mind was not firing with hundreds of thoughts or a mile-long to-do list. It was just… quiet.

I can't tell you how long I sat there perfectly still, staring off into space with that feeling, but it was quite a while. This was not normal for me. I rarely sat still—and certainly *never* like this.

Eventually I realized a significant amount of time had passed. It was growing close to midnight.

I got up, locked the door, and turned the heat down. Without even realizing it, I carried the cordless phone to my bedroom instead of putting it back on the charger. I climbed into bed fully dressed—again, something completely unlike me.

Within about an hour, the phone rang.

Instantly, I knew something was terribly wrong.

It was my dad. His words were barely understandable, but I heard enough.

Nathan—my brother—had died.

I threw the covers back, slid into my shoes, and ran straight to my dad's house, just a couple minutes away. I kept hoping this was all some terrible dream.

The days, weeks, and years after what I experienced that night weighed heavily on me. I didn't understand what I had felt, but I knew it was *something*—something that left me with confusion and fear that was mingled alongside my grief.

While my brother was in deep distress, my spirit had sensed it.

Had I known then what I know now, instead of sitting in that paralysis, I would have prayed. Even if I didn't know who or what it was for, I would have recognized *the need*. What I experienced that night was discernment—a spiritual gift I wouldn't understand for decades.

The confusion shaped me—but it did not own me.
The fear influenced me—but it did not define me.
The witchcraft pressed in—but it did not overcome me.

My lack of knowledge was used to twist what God intended for good. If fear surrounded my experiences, I would never see them as coming from my Heavenly Father. And if I doubted their source, it would drive distance and separation from God.

If the supernatural felt dangerous, it could keep me from stepping into the calling God had placed on my life. He used my grandmother's card readings as a reference point and the spiritual heaviness of my childhood as a comparison. He used my confusion and lack of godly guidance as a weapon against me.

What he didn't understand was—he could confuse me—but he could never cancel what God had placed inside me. "For God's gifts and His call are irrevocable." (Romans 11:29)

Clearly now, all of these experiences I couldn't explain are now clear—they were gifts of discernment.
They were signs of purpose.
They were signs that God was awakening my spirit.

In my mistrust, God waited not with frustration, but with a quiet invitation for me to reach toward Him and draw closer. He didn't force understanding on me. He didn't rush me into maturity. He had a plan with perfect timing.

God would untangle what I feared. He would eventually separate the counterfeit from the calling. He would show me that what I carried wasn't a burden. When my confirmation would finally come, it would be a memory forever etched in my heart and mind—marked by the sound of *Amazing Grace.*

A Purpose

For years, I believed my exposure to darkness disqualified me. I felt unworthy. I assumed the enemy's presence in my early life meant I had been marked by something unholy and abandoned by God. Even later in life, in my early walk with Him, I struggled with that belief.

But what God would later show me changed everything.

The very things meant to intimidate me became the very things God redeemed and used as a weapon—my weapon—the very thing the enemy had feared all along.

When you've seen both the authentic and the counterfeit up close, you recognize the differences immediately. When you've felt the heaviness of darkness, you don't mistake it for light. When you've watched the enemy operate, you can discern his voice before he even speaks.

"For we are not ignorant of his devices." (2 Corinthians 2:11)

"For our struggle is not against flesh and blood…" (Ephesians 6:12). Long before I understood what to call them, I had encountered those principalities. I felt their pressure, saw their influence, and watched how quietly they moved.

The girl who once felt tainted is now led by the Holy Spirit, with Jesus holding her hand. What once brought fear has been replaced with the authority "to walk on snakes and scorpions… and over all the power of the enemy" (Luke 10:19). The same power that raised Jesus from the dead now lives in me.

The one who once hid her gift now embraces it.

What the enemy thought would mark me, God turned into training—training to recognize deception, discern spirits, and step into places where darkness still tries to hide.

Now, at forty-five years old, I walk with confidence—not in myself, but in the One who kept me, redeemed me, and equipped me to stand against the very darkness that once tried to destroy me.

Familiarity

Sometimes evil and darkness slip in quietly—through patterns, atmospheres, and unspoken rules that shape you long before you understand what they mean. For me, darkness didn't feel like darkness at all. It felt normal. It felt like the air I breathed.

The pressure I carried was something I accepted without question. I learned early how to live inside silence.

Growing up surrounded by spiritual confusion, emotional instability, and unspoken expectations, you don't recognize them to be harmful. You simply adapt. You survive. Living in the shadows becomes normal—and when it's normal long enough, it begins to feel safe. —That was me.

Even before adolescence, I was becoming "me" without ever really knowing who I was. I stayed quiet when something hurt. I said yes when my spirit was whispering no. I allowed boundaries to be crossed that I didn't yet know how to hold. I shaped myself into whatever kept the peace—whatever made me likable, whatever kept the atmosphere calm. I had mastered minimization.

From a young age, I could read a room. I could sense tension before a word was spoken. I could feel the emotional temperature the moment I walked through the door.

To avoid conflict.
To stay quiet.
To stay out of the way.

None of those things were conscious decisions. These became instincts—instincts shaped by years of experience.

I didn't recognize the enemy's influence because it had been woven into my life so quietly and so consistently that it simply felt familiar.

Darkness doesn't feel dangerous when it's all you've ever known. It feels like home.

Roots

As I grew older, the responsibilities I carried as a child didn't fade—they only grew heavier. What had started as small burdens quietly turned into expectations I never questioned. I learned to be strong because I believed I had no other choice. I learned to be independent because, somewhere deep inside, I was convinced no one was coming to the rescue.

I carried burdens that should have never belonged to a child. And in those quiet places of my mind, the enemy whispered lies that sounded an awful lot like truth:

"You can only rely on yourself"—this would be replaced with *"You don't need anyone."*

"You have no room to fall apart"

Those thoughts didn't feel like lies at the time. They felt practical. Necessary. They felt like the rules of survival.

Little by little, those lies began shaping how I saw myself and the world around me. I wore strength like armor, believing it was the only thing keeping everything from collapsing. I didn't realize then that what felt like strength was slowly becoming a set of chains—chains God would one day break.

I was pulled inward—toward a life mostly lived inside my own thoughts where my fears stayed locked away. I didn't know how to talk about spiritual things. I didn't discuss my pain and hurt. I didn't know who to trust with my vulnerability.

So, I stayed silent. Silence was bondage wrapped around my life.

But even then—when I didn't recognize Him—God was there.
In the shadows, in the confusion, in the darkness, He was there.
His seed of light—planted long before—remained buried but alive,
waiting for the right moment to grow.

I didn't recognize His voice yet. I didn't understand His pursuit.
But He already knew every place I had hidden my fears. He knew
every question I had buried and every experience I was too afraid to
speak about. And deeper than anything else—an ache to be loved.

Marriage

I would enter marriage five days after turning twenty-one with an eighteen-month-old child. I had grown up quickly and believed I was more mature than my years.

Responsibility didn't intimidate me. Strength and self-reliance were my identity, and asking for help simply was not in my vocabulary.

But underneath that strength was still the little girl who had learned early to stay quiet, and small—believing belonging had to be earned.

"Train up a child in the way he should go." (Proverbs 22:6)

Long before I understood the weight of that verse, I was trained in self-survival. I knew how to adapt and carry responsibility, but I had never learned how to rest or what healthy love was supposed to look like.

"Love is patient. Love is kind." (1 Corinthians 13:4–5)
Love, to me, had always felt conditional—something fragile that had to be earned and carefully maintained. My heart simply trusted what felt familiar. "The heart is deceitful above all things." (Jeremiah 17:9)

Mine certainly was.

I wasn't consulting God. I was building from longing rather than obedience or spiritual wisdom. I can clearly see the truth of Scripture: "Unless the Lord builds the house, they who build it labor in vain." (Psalm 127:1).

Sadly, I didn't know how to be loved, receive love, or how to trust love.

For a girl who had spent most of her life feeling unwanted, the idea of stability and family felt like enough. At the time, it seemed like the answer to everything I thought I had been missing.

And now I was a mother. Giving my child the things I felt I had never received weighed heavily on my heart.

But that still wasn't enough.
Not for a covenant.
Not for a lifetime.
Not for the spiritual weight marriage carries.

Still, I stepped into it anyway. Standing outside the county courthouse before an ordained minister I had never met—a man named Leroy in green alligator boots—I entered what would become a twenty-year marriage already wounded and already weary. It wasn't a day of celebration but rather a day of legality. Somewhere deep inside, I had quietly accepted that this might simply be as good as life was ever going to get.

Patterns

What followed was not sudden. It was gradual. Quiet. Because of my lack of healing, I adjusted to meet everyone else's needs. Emptiness will always settle for less than God's best. I lived inside the same emotional strongholds learned in childhood: the fear of abandonment, the pressure to be "enough," the belief that peace was derived from silence.

Outwardly, I was determined to curate the image of the dream—a perfect marriage, a perfect family. I was hyper-attentive to how everything looked from the outside. I was not going to give anyone the opportunity to label the life I had built as a failure. I believed everything had to appear as flowing flawlessly. It had to be Facebook-worthy. I see now how that mindset drove so much unnecessary tension.

Internally, I carried unrest. A strain that never quite settled. I was firm in my belief being a good wife meant submission. It meant being the glue that holds it all together. Managing the details. Keeping peace at all costs. My norm became tolerating way beyond boundaries I had no clue how to set.

There were moments when the pressure became too heavy for me to carry. Something in me finally would push back. Those breaking points were few and far between. They didn't happen over small inconveniences or minor frustrations. I had mastered the art of picking my battles—and truthfully, for nineteen of those twenty years, I hardly picked any at all.

I told myself silence was strength and restraint was maturity— that swallowing my disappointment made me a good wife. I let myself settle for the bare minimum and called it enough

I did not want to be "that woman." The woman who nags. Those women described as difficult, dramatic, impossible to please. The woman whose name is brought up in conversations with that famous five-letter word—*aka female dog*, followed by eye rolls and sarcastic remarks—the kind I could frequently overhear in the garage when some spoke about their own significant others.

Somewhere I had picked up the mentality, that a good wife stays silent.

She adjusts.

She tolerates.

She glosses things over.

She *is expected* to carry emotional burdens without complaint.

And I felt I needed to stay within those lines.

I minimized what hurt. I convinced myself I could handle it. And when I finally did speak—naming the hurt, naming what wasn't working, asking for change—it was because I had reached a breaking point. A place of crushing.

I would hope, quietly, there would be change. But what followed was a familiar cycle. Eventually, I would find myself right back at the same breaking point—the very place I had promised I would never return to. "Hope deferred makes the heart sick." (Proverbs 13:12) Without healing, wounds don't disappear. They repeat.

God's design for marriage is sacred. It is meant to reflect covenant, unity, and love rooted in Him. I now understand that I entered that marriage driven more by longing than by God's leading. I wanted stability. I wanted belonging. I wanted something to feel secure. My desire wasn't wrong—but my foundation was. God was not at the center.

God has allowed me to see my own wounds more clearly that I brought into that marriage. Not to shame me. Not to condemn me. But to heal me. Healing is not about passing blame. It is about humbly recognizing what within you accepted patterns that were never aligned with God's best.

There were areas in me that were unhealed—fear of abandonment, a tendency toward silence, an overdeveloped sense of responsibility. Those internal patterns shaped how I responded, what I tolerated, and how I navigated conflict. I cannot control another person's choices, but I am responsible for my own choices and growth.

Without healing, we repeat what feels familiar—even when it isn't healthy. Familiarity can masquerade as comfort. But with healing comes clarity. With clarity comes change. And with change, cycles can finally be broken.

And yet, those years were not wasted.

God wastes nothing.

Even in a season when I had drifted far from Him—when I was not seeking Him the way I should have—His grace and mercy were still present. I may not have recognized His hand at the time, but He never withdrew it. He was steady when I was not.

In that relationship, God entrusted me with two of the greatest gifts of my life—my children. Whatever else that season held, this remains undeniable: they were intentional blessings placed into my care.

"Children are a heritage from the Lord." (Psalm 127:3)

They were my anchors during storms I didn't know how to navigate. They were light in seasons that felt dim. They gave me purpose when I felt lost and strength when I felt weak. Loving them awakened something in me—a tenderness, a protectiveness, a depth of love I had never fully known before.

Through them, God was shaping me—even when I didn't yet understand I was being shaped.

They were never accidents of circumstance. They were gifts of grace. For that alone, I can say with certainty—those years were not wasted.

44

Motherhood and Marriage

Motherhood is beautiful—a love so fierce and unexplainable it feels etched into the soul long before birth. But by the time I became a mother, I was already exhausted. Not physically, but emotionally and spiritually.

At twenty years old, I was a new and unwed mother living in sin—trying to nurture when no one had nurtured me. Trying to love while I was still learning what love even was.

Marriage finally came when my daughter was eighteen months old, but it did not lift the burden my spirit carried. In the moments I needed support most, I often felt alone. I stayed strong by burying the grief of unspoken and unmet needs. Loneliness turned into disappointment, and disappointment slowly hardened into resentment toward everyone I felt had failed me.

There were quiet, private moments when I felt myself drowning. Sometimes the strain became so heavy I wondered if this was all my life would ever be. I felt trapped inside a covenant that was slowly suffocating me. I did what I had always done.

I stayed silent.

I did not expect motherhood and marriage to feel so heavy. I did not anticipate how draining it would be to pour from a place that was already empty.

But I didn't tell anyone. I was alone with the fear of possible judgment—the fear that needing support meant failure. So, I buried everything and kept going.

And yet, inside, something was unraveling.

Something was breaking.

Something was slowly dying.

And I had no idea how to stop it.

Mothering While Motherless

My parents divorced when I was eight years old. That alone changes the landscape of a child's life. The one person who had filled that motherly space for me—my grandmother—passed away when I was twenty-one. When she left, something in my world shifted yet again.

I was raising a baby of my own.

There was no tribe of women around me. No group of mothers to lean on, no wise voices to call when I felt overwhelmed or unsure. My circle had grown small over the years—partly by circumstance and partly by design. Trust didn't come easy for me, and leaving my baby with anyone else simply wasn't a possibility.

Which meant there I was, trying to mother a child when I had never truly been mothered myself. There was no safe place to fall apart when everything felt too heavy. No gentle voice speaking life into me when doubt crept in. No one stepping in with nurturing, comfort, or rest.

I mothered the only way I knew how.

From wounds.

Yet God places something inside a mother that rises up when her child arrives. Those instincts—the ones only heaven can explain—became my guide.

I loved my children fiercely. I gave everything I had, even on days and years when my own cup was bone dry.

I was determined to give my children what I had longed for.

But if I'm honest, part of me was also chasing the appearance of perfection. Somewhere deep inside, perfection felt safer than admitting parts of my life were still broken.

Back then, I didn't understand something I know now.

Love does not require perfection.

Working Mother

I stepped away from the family business and into the corporate workforce. The financial need was real, and on paper it made sense. I was also ready for a home of our own, as we were living with my in-laws.

My daughter and I would share that first day—my first day in the workforce and her first day of preschool.

But in reality, the separation carried a heaviness I wasn't prepared for. The ache of leaving her was real. The guilt hit hard.

She loved her school days with other children to play with. For me, every goodbye felt heavier than it should have, as if I were choosing survival over presence.

I grieved the hours I was missing out on. But I told myself I was doing what I had to do. Emotionally, I would feel another fracture—another place where love and absence collided.

I felt like I needed to make up for lost time. Saturdays became ours—girls' day. Every Saturday was special. They were sacred. Movies. Nails. Playgrounds. Anything that gave us time that was just ours. I wanted our bond to feel secure. I carried a quiet fear of being replaced—through the separation. So, I overcompensated.

I made sure she knew I was present. I made sure she felt chosen—the priority. I tried to create memories strong enough to anchor us.

I wasn't just protecting time. I was protecting against loss. I didn't realize how much of that fear came from my younger self.

I worked. I mothered. I managed the household. I kept everything moving and intact.

Loss of a Child

I had lived through losses, however, when you lose a child that is a different kind of loss.

Being five and a half months pregnant with my second child, Knox, I drove myself to the hospital on a Saturday afternoon after bleeding had begun. I knew something was wrong. A woman knows. A mother knows. Deep inside, I felt—dread knowing something had changed.

Sitting in that hospital room, my fear was confirmed. I was told my child who had been active in my belly the night before was now gone. The hope and excitement for the future was now gone.

No explanation.

No medical reason—just that his heart stopped.

Silence and a void where life had so recently been.

My body had already recognized this loss and was starting to respond. In situations like this, there is no concern for the baby's health during labor, because there is no life on the other end. Medication was pushed aggressively to intensify contractions, to bring an ending where there would be no beginning. There is no relief—only a process.

I endured hours of labor that stretched into the next night.

I labored knowing there would be no reward waiting on the other side.

No relief wrapped in celebration. No cry filling the room.

I labored knowing this pain would not bring life.

I would never have an opportunity to hear him cry or see him grow. Never a first step or the sound of his voice.

After he was born, I tried to savor those moments I did have with him. Holding his tiny lifeless body, I etched his face into my mind. As most mothers eagerly do, I counted his ten fingers and ten toes with only sadness.

The room held no joy, no celebration.
Only silence. Only grief.

Every second that passed was one less second remaining with him. I watched the clock on the wall knowing soon the time I had with him would be gone.

This child I knew and loved would forever remain a memory of what could have been—a piece of my heart torn away, a chapter that ended before it ever had the chance to begin.

A decision still had to be made. Early in labor, the hospital staff explained my options—burial or donation. I knew where my finances were. I managed them on a week-to-week basis very carefully. There were no funds available for any celebration for this child that never had a chance at a life. With a heavy and crushing heart, a decision was made—shaped not only by finances, but also by the presence and perspectives of others in the room.

Even though others were at the hospital, I felt alone in my mother's grief. Alone in my questions. Alone in the ache that settled into my bones.

Why this was happening to *me—why my child.*

Left Behind

As I moved into the wheelchair, the pain in my heart became overwhelming—so intense it felt as though I could barely breathe. It was time to leave the hospital. Each breath came strained, as if my body itself was resisting the reality of having to leave.

I couldn't speak. I was afraid that if I opened my mouth, I would lose total control. It took all I had to maintain composure, as my world was collapsing.

But the pain continued to intensify.

Grief, disbelief, anger—all those emotions were rushing in, and they were totally debilitating.

It continued to rise—steady, consuming, unrelenting—as the hospital doors came into view.

With every inch closer to the exit, I felt my opportunity to speak slipping away. The ache in my chest deepened. The decision had already been made, yet my heart was still fighting it.

The weight of it pressed into my bones.

Those final moments stretched thin—seconds that felt suspended in time. My mind raced with questions I didn't dare say out loud.

How could I change my mind now? How would we afford it?

I didn't speak.

That silence is something my mother's heart will always regret. I carry the burden of what cannot be undone.

My Knox was left behind.

A piece of me remained inside those walls, beneath a heat lamp.

Torn in Two

Prior to the pain and loss of losing my son—just months earlier, in February—my nineteen-year-old brother, Nathan, had died by suicide.

That kind of loss doesn't arrive quietly. It crashes in and rearranges everything. The phone call in the middle of the night. The total disbelief. The way time seemed to move and stand still all at once. One moment he was here, and the next there was a silence that would never be filled again.

I had been forced to explain death to my four-year-old daughter in those weeks that had followed. I was still trying to wrap my own mind around it, and yet I had to put words to something even adults struggle to understand.

She asked questions over and over.

Where did he go?

Why did he die?

Can that happen to us?

Her innocent little mind was trying to make sense of something far too heavy for her years. I had to be quick on my feet. I reassured her that death came much later in life—that she wasn't going to die, and neither were her dad or I. Not for a very, very long time.

I said those words trying to quiet her fears, as well as some of my own.

Now here it was—June 2004. I was in the hospital. In labor. In delivery. Faced with decisions no mother should ever have to make. On top of that, I realized I was about to have to explain death again.

Only this time, it was her brother.

She had been so excited. She talked about helping. About being a big sister. There were tiny clothes folded and waiting. There were plans. There was expectation. Now there was silence.

My body was actively responding with labor while my heart was shattering. I was a mother drowning in grief for my son while still carrying the ache of losing my brother.

How was I going to explain this loss when I was just trying to survive myself. At that same time, I had to gather whatever strength and sensibility I had left to try to protect and comfort my living child.

I didn't feel equipped. I didn't feel strong. I felt split in half. Torn in two.

In desperation, I swore the adults around me to secrecy. I told them I would explain it away—that the doctors had made a mistake, that there hadn't really been a baby. That was why I was in the hospital.

It sounds irrational now. But grief makes you grasp for anything that feels survivable. I thought if I could shield her from the truth, maybe I could shield her from the pain. But truth has a way of slipping through the cracks.

It wasn't long before she overheard a conversation she wasn't meant to hear. Just like that, the secret unraveled.

She found out she had a brother.

A conversation I wasn't ready for. A moment I wasn't prepared to navigate. Her little face searching for answers I still didn't have.

That wound, once forced open, eventually became a place of honesty. Over time, transparency brought a layer of healing I hadn't expected. No more secrecy. No more pretending. No more carrying it alone.

God would not allow his life, no matter how short it was, to be erased. Even a life that never took a breath left a mark. That mark mattered.

The grief was stacked so high I began to question everything.

Loss after loss.

Grief after grief.

It felt like a pattern. A cycle.

I wondered if God was punishing me. If I was cursed. If something dark had attached itself to my family line and followed me into adulthood.

I knew curses were real.

I knew spiritual darkness was real.

I knew evil existed.

I felt like it had wrapped itself around me, tightening its grip.

But even then—in the grief, in the confusion, in the silence when answers didn't come—God was near. I just didn't know it yet.

Emotions Collide

A year after losing my son, I was already emotionally gone from my marriage. I didn't say it out loud—I didn't have the courage, or the support—but inside, I wanted out.

I had felt an emotional loneliness. I didn't yet have the words to explain it, only the feeling of being undervalued and unsupported. I was unsure of how to express what I needed. The distance wasn't loud or dramatic—it was subtle, steady, and deeply isolating.

I was exhausted.
Empty.
Done.

And then, in the middle of all of that, I found out I was pregnant. I was carrying a child while carrying the weight of a marriage I no longer wanted to be in and the guilt of the timing of a child coming into this environment.
It wasn't planned.
It wasn't expected.
And it certainly wasn't the timing I wanted.

I remember staring at the third positive pregnancy test and the tears rolling, feeling emotions collide inside me—love, dread, and fear.
Love, because motherhood had awakened the softest parts of me. For the first time, I had experienced true love through my children.

Absolutely no doubt—I already loved this child. I wanted this child.

Dread, because I knew I was bringing a child into a marriage that I felt was already breaking.

Fear, because I knew the pain of losing a child and my heart could not withstand another blow.

Buckling

Internally, I was emotionally fragile—but externally everyone would only see a woman on a mission—steady—controlled, and focused. The pregnancy was internally a battle of fear. There were complications from the beginning. Uncertainty at every appointment. Bouts of preterm labor and weeks of bed rest.

Christmas Eve and Christmas Day were close calls. We held on. Just a few days after Christmas at thirty-seven weeks, I delivered a beautiful blue-eyed baby boy—my gift from God.

The pregnancy had been difficult, but it was nothing compared to the years that followed. As a newborn, there were complications which would lead to nine surgeries in three years.

The memory of my son's first surgery still haunts me—standing outside the operating room doors.

He was an infant. His tiny arms were strapped to boards to keep him from pulling at the tubing. I could not bear the thought of him without warmth and love wrapped around him. I refused to let him lay alone in that hospital crib, so large it seemed to swallow him. I held him carefully, working around the boards and the tubes that ran from his little body.

I spent the entire morning with him in my arms—watching his every breath, tracing the outline of his face, gently touching his soft cotton hair—unsure what this day would mean for my son and for our family. I refused to lose a single second of being able to hold my precious baby boy. I savored each second as if it might be my last. I watched the clock—every tick louder than the one before—knowing the moment was drawing near. I would have to hand him over to strangers who would try to fix what was threatening his life.

I didn't want to let go. I wanted to protect him from everything he had already endured—and from everything that was still to come.

But I couldn't.

When it was time, I carried him to the operating room doors. I didn't rush. I couldn't. I wanted to stretch those final seconds in my arms for as long as possible. I pressed my cheek against his head and whispered words only he could hear. My arms held him tightly, but my heart was already bracing for the moment I would have to let go. When the nurse reached for him, my hands trembled and my body shuttered. The tears I had been fighting finally fell.

And when those doors closed between us, my knees buckled.

Not out of faith in a loving God—but out of fear.

Out of helplessness. Out of the unbearable ache of watching my child suffer and not understanding why it had to be him—My tiny baby.

I had so many questions:

What did I do wrong?

Was this my punishment because of my previous dread?

Why would an innocent baby have to endure so much?

Why would God allow this?

I wasn't strong in that moment. I wasn't full of trust. I wasn't quoting Scripture or standing in confidence.

I didn't understand how to call on God to carry me through that moment. I had no idea I could speak His name over my child for protection or healing. It had never crossed my mind to pray for His divine touch or to understand the power of a community of believers standing in prayer.

I had not yet learned that "where two or three are gathered in My name, there am I among them." (Matthew 18:20) or discovered that "The prayer of a righteous person is powerful and effective." (James 5:16) I had no idea God moved through community—through intercession, through agreement, through shared faith.

All I knew was I felt utterly alone and completely helpless.

I was a mother breaking under the weight of worry and fear for her child. A woman who hadn't yet discovered that "The Spirit helps us in our weakness" (Romans 8:26), or that I could "approach the throne of grace with confidence." (Hebrews 4:16)

But in that moment of fear and grief, even without words, my tears and crushed spirit were heard by a loving God.

Survival

I was twenty-five with two children. One of them needed critical medical care that was vital to his survival. There wasn't time to fall apart. Survival mode doesn't look chaotic. It looks like competence. Like strength. Like a mother who appears to have it all together.

On the inside, it is something else. It is living from appointment to appointment. It is measuring time in procedures and recovery windows. It is keeping a hospital bag packed. It is knowing in-depth the layout of the local pediatric hospital.

Your body and mind stay alert—your mind runs scenarios before doctors finish sentences. You do all you can to avoid adverse outcomes. You learn to swallow your fear and push through for your child and your family.

You function. You organize schedules and medications, track follow-ups, and advocate. Your sleep becomes shallow. Joy becomes cautious. You become efficient at crisis.

All of this unfolded while I had another child who stood on the sidelines. Another little heart watching. Waiting. Needing.

I was dividing myself constantly—one child's care tied to survival, the other trying to understand why she had to take a back seat. I tried to be everything for both.

There were moments I knew I was stretched too thin.

Love was never divided. But my presence was.

Somehow, I managed a full-time job with mandatory overtime while running on fumes. My children needed me—but I needed that job. The medical insurance my job provided was not optional; it was critical. Also, so was the income that kept our household afloat.

There was no choice that didn't cost something. Somewhere along the way, I changed. My personality grew less welcoming. I had no margin, for anything extra—or anyone. I kept moving. Managing calendars. Clocking in and clocking out. Sitting in hospital rooms after long shifts. Coming home to homework, dinner, laundry, and exhaustion.

Living in survival mode has a cost. It hardens you. It numbs places that used to respond. It teaches you how to endure—but not how to rest.

When the crisis finally slowed, my body did not know how to. I had lived braced for years. There was no full exhale. No space to collapse. The quiet moments, I stayed alert—waiting for the next complication of life to hit.

Motherhood—Now Versus Then

Motherhood—I didn't always do it right. Some moments I would relive in a heartbeat; others I would totally rewrite if I could. I tried to do my best with what I knew and understood at the time.

I see now what I couldn't see in those breaking moments of motherhood—they were invitations to call on God. I had lived where fear was louder than faith, pain louder than prayer, and confusion louder than confidence.

I didn't understand that I could cry out to Him. That I could speak His name over my children. That a mother's intercession carries weight in heaven.

Now I do.

If I could step back into that hospital hallway—to the moment my knees buckled and my heart burned with questions and anger—I would fall to the floor in faith. I would call on the name of Jesus, speaking life over my son. I would declare God's protection with authority. I would not stand alone. I would call on my brothers and sisters to pray beside me.

Now I understand: prayer is not a last resort—it is a daily relationship requirement. Fear is not proof of God's absence—it is often the place where His presence is most needed.

I cannot rewrite those early years. But I do live differently now.

Today, even from a distance, I intercede for my children with a boldness I once lacked. I speak God's Word over them. I cover them in prayers they may never know about. I fight battles in the spirit on their behalf—not because I am strong, but because I finally know the One who is.

What once felt like failure has become fuel. What once felt like fear has become faith. Those moments did not disqualify me. They prepared me.

Prayer—it is daily.
For my children.
For my family.
For all that I love.

Spiritual Paralysis

The marriage I was in at the time didn't just repeat the patterns of my childhood. Instead of healing my wounds, that season felt like it deepened them. The same elements from childhood resurfaced. I was careful with my words. Careful with my tone. Careful with timing. I measured conversations before they ever left my mouth. I watched moods. I anticipated tension before it arrived. I could feel a shift in the room before anyone spoke.

"A gentle tongue is a tree of life, but perverseness in it breaks the spirit." (Proverbs 15:4) My spirit was breaking.

I couldn't recognize it then. I thought I was just being patient. I thought I was being mature. I thought I was showing love. But I was losing pieces of myself—not all at once, but in small, daily compromises.

Compromises of peace and confidence. Somewhere in all of that, I stopped hearing my own voice.

There were attempts I would make to draw close to God. I would visit church occasionally in hopes of giving my children that experience—hoping they would encounter something I still questioned and struggled to understand myself.

But every attempt I made to draw near to Him felt harder than it should have. Not dramatic. Not explosive. Just…blocked.

I would try to carve out a quiet moment to open my Bible, but the words might as well have been written in another language. I would read a chapter and retain nothing. I would start in Genesis and feel overwhelmed before I even made it through a few pages.

I felt stupid. I would close it quietly, almost embarrassed—like I had failed some kind of test. I would tell myself I would try again later.

Later never came.

Life distractions would rise up. Conflict would surface. Responsibilities would pile on. Or I would simply feel too emotionally drained to even try.

Occasionally I would feel a gentle nudge—something stirring inside me that I couldn't quite explain. It would be quickly replaced with a thought of discouragement. A distraction. A whisper that made me feel foolish for even trying.

Trying felt difficult when I was just trying to survive life. Life would take precedence and the church visits would subside as quickly as they began. The Bible would be put back in a drawer.

I had never been introduced to the difference between religion and relationship. In my mind there was only rigid religion rules which represented Christianity. I thought this was the only way—but this thinking only led to frustration and distance.

Yet even in that distance, something inside me would periodically feel the pull. Honestly, I didn't know Him and barely knew any scripture at all. But I still believed He mattered.

I eventually started a tradition in our home on Christmas Eve of taking communion—yes, even in seasons when we weren't living right. And to be clear, I wasn't walking some middle ground of faith during that time… internally my faith was still very deeply questioned. I wrestled with what I believed, and I wasn't sure where I stood with God.

But even in the middle of that uncertainty, there was something in me that felt led to remember Jesus… to pause and recognize the reason for the season. As a mother, it mattered to me that my children knew

Christmas wasn't just about lights and gifts—it was about the birth of Jesus.

There was no sanctuary or pastor leading us. Technically there was no prayer with it. It was just a momma and her kids standing in our kitchen or sitting in the living room, giving honor to Him with some crackers and juice.

In complete honesty, I didn't fully understand the biblical expectations of communion or *all* of the meaning behind it. It would be a while before I would figure all those things out...

But this simple gesture inside our home was effort. I believe God saw my heart, and rejoiced in those moments. I pray with everything in me that this simple act planted seeds in my children.

Even when I felt distant from Him, when confusion clouded my understanding, something deep within me still knew. My seed had been planted long before. And even when I wandered, that seed was still alive.

I now see something from all those moments in my life. If I had discovered who I was in Christ during that season—if I had fully grasped the authority and identity available to me—if I had fully grasped the authority and identity available to me—the enemy would have lost his foothold. His strategy was always confusion. Distraction. Emotional instability. Creating just enough noise to keep me spiritually paralyzed.

And paralysis leaves you stuck—no growth or understanding.

But even in that paralysis, God never left me—even when I didn't understand His Word, His presence, or closed the Bible in frustration.

Presence and Protection

There were moments—quiet, subtle moments—when His holy
presence broke through the heaviness. Moments when He held me and
pushed back against the lies.

One moment in 2013 stands out like a sharp edge in my
memory—the moment I knew I could not continue living in what had
become the norm. I was so deflated, so worn down, so emotionally
exhausted that something inside me felt like it was collapsing. I knew
that if something didn't change, I feared I would never know peace.

Part of that realization came from looking back at the home I grew
up in. My grandparents' home had been filled with emotional
unpredictability. My grandmother spent her entire life hoping she
would one day have peace in her home. When my grandfather passed
away, she followed him very unexpectedly just four days later.

She waited for peace that never fully came. That truth hit me with
a force I wasn't prepared for. It shook me. It terrified me. I did not
want that to be my story. I didn't want to spend my life waiting for a
peace that would never arrive.

A vacation had just ended. I should have been ecstatic,
invigorated, and refreshed. The social media pictures told one story,
but my heart was living another. The trip was not what I had hoped
for—but deep down, it was what I had come to expect.

On the drive home from Florida, I barely spoke ten words. I
wasn't angry. I was numb.

Arriving home, hopelessness and exhaustion pressed in so heavily that I found myself longing for an escape as I sat alone in my office. Not because I wanted my life to end, but because I didn't know how to keep living at that level.

In that dark moment, God placed a barrier of protection around me.

My baby brother had died by suicide. I have firsthand experience with the layers of grief it leaves behind. Remembering it stopped me in my tracks.

Just returning from vacation my children had went straight to their grandparents' house to spend the night. In that moment of struggle, my blessings—my children—came to mind with a force that felt like divine intervention. Their faces. Their futures. Their need for me.

That was enough to pull me back from the edge—an edge I was just a hair away from crossing.

In that moment, something settled in my spirit with absolute clarity: when my life ends, it will not be by my own hand. If my peace was ever going to exist, something had to change.

For the first time, I welcomed the thought of a divorce; I no longer feared it. It wasn't rebellion. It wasn't impulsive. I didn't have the full picture yet, but I knew this: I would not live the rest of my life the same way my grandmother had—I would not die waiting for peace.

I would fight for it.

That night became a turning point. What I didn't know then was that the divorce I longed for—the peace my spirit desperately desired—would not come for many more years. There was still a cancer battle that would have to be faced and managed through.

At the time, that delay felt like more torment. More waiting. More confusion. It felt almost cruel, and it stirred anger toward God. It felt like punishment.

I now see it for what it truly was—part of a purpose and a plan.

Unraveling

Eventually the end of that marriage—and confrontation of a generational cycle would come. God wasn't withholding freedom. He was preparing me for it. He was positioning my heart, my mind, and my spirit for a breaking point.

The unraveling didn't happen overnight. It came slowly, through years of erosion and through choices. An affair would shift everything. There was no coming back from that. It forced me to face what I had already known: a fractured foundation will only continue to fracture more.

The affair was not rebellion for rebellion's sake. It rose from brokenness—from feeling unseen, unheard, and undervalued. But brokenness does not excuse sin.

What felt like the worst mistake of my life became a mirror. I would no longer pretend. I stood in the fact: This chapter was over. This was ending.

The door was going to close on that marriage—not because God could not have restored it. Let me be clear—*Anything* is possible with God. The Bible clearly outlines it. I also fully believe it. But restoration would have required three hearts aligned toward the same purpose— the husband, the wife, and God at the center.

At that time, my heart was not aligned. I chose to step away. Not because redemption was impossible, but because I did not desire it. I was not fighting for healing. I was fighting for closure.

My heart had hardened in places I did not want to examine. Instead of asking God to restore what was broken, I shut down the possibility and convinced myself it was easier to start over than to rebuild what I felt was beyond repair.

Years later, I see the weight of that decision—the pain, the pride, the exhaustion, the woundedness that shaped it all. I also see this: even when I refused restoration, God did not refuse me.

He allowed the consequences.
He allowed the unraveling.

In the shame, in the confusion, in the collapse of everything I had built—He remained steady.

The affair was never God-ordained and certainly not His plan. It was my participation in sin. Every sin carries pain—unfortunately, in this case, the pain reached far beyond just my own. But even there, grace was waiting.

What was meant for destruction, God would not waste. He did not excuse my choices—but He refuse to abandon me to them.

Uncertainty

Divorce is hard no matter the circumstances. Mine became something I never could have imagined. Something that was unheard of. Unthinkable.

I walked full force into a divorce at the exact same time the world was walking into a pandemic.

The timing felt unreal—almost cruel. One kind of uncertainty would have been enough. But I was handed two. The uncertainty of a marriage ending alongside of uncertainty of the world shutting down.

Courthouses closed.

Processes stalled.

Phones calls without any answers.

Everything around the world seemed to pause—except the stress inside my chest.

The news talked about fear and isolation like it was something new. Inside my home, I was already living it. I watched the world count cases and lockdowns while I counted days… waiting for movement, waiting for resolution, waiting for something to give.

I couldn't believe what was happening. Just when I thought there might be a path forward, everything slowed to a crawl. My life felt suspended in midair.

What should have taken a few months turned into three long years. Three years stuck in limbo. Three years waiting for the chance to rebuild while the whole world felt like it was coming undone.

All that time, my own family was unraveling right there in the middle of it.

Holidays became heavier. There was no clean break, no clear next step—just waiting. Waiting for paperwork. Waiting for dates. Waiting for a system that wasn't even functioning.

The world called it quarantine.

I called it torture.

Every plan I had for "after this is over" kept getting pushed further out. With every delay, it felt like pieces of my life were stretching thinner and thinner.

The waiting was breaking me and my family.

"Be still, and know that I am God." (Psalm 46:10) That verse became a quiet whisper in a season where stillness was debilitating. It was a strange kind of isolation—not just the physical distance everyone was living through, but the emotional distance of walking through one of the hardest seasons of my life without the ability to move forward.

Everywhere I turned, there was uncertainty.

And yet, in that tension, in the delay, God was silently working. What felt like a setback was actually protection. What felt like a pause was actually preparation. This chaos was actually God holding the pieces until I was prepared enough to pick them up. "And the God of all grace… will Himself restore, confirm, strengthen, and establish you." (1 Peter 5:10)

I didn't see it then, but now I understand: The delay wasn't punishment. It was divine timing.

He was going to restore what the locust had eaten. He had a perfect plan that included pieces which were not quite ready for His perfect timing.

The world was shaking, but God was steady. My life felt uncertain, but His plan was not. "He will be the stability of your times…" (Isaiah 33:6) Even through the stress and chaos, in the three-year delay, He was still there.

The Plan

In December of 2020, my divorce was a year and a half into the process, and my world felt volatile. While the world was in the middle of a pandemic, full of uncertainty, Mark entered my life. I had known of him from a distance for most of my life.

He was close with my uncles, familiar to my family, and fourteen years older than me. Our paths had brushed past each other in our small town, but never in a way that hinted at what God had intended.

In that season, there was a shift starting. Mark didn't come into my life loudly or dramatically. He came quietly—steady, grounded, and safe. Instantly I was at home in his presence. Mark would become a rock in the middle of my unsteady world. Someone who would speak calm into the places where fear had lived for so long. I didn't know or could even fathom it then, but God had created us for one another.

Mark didn't come to manipulate me. He didn't try to fix me. He didn't try to fill the void. He came just to love me.

Mark understood the weight on my shoulders as he had encountered a devastating divorce just two years prior. He didn't try to be anything more than who he was, which was exactly what I needed.

Even though Mark had walked through his own life challenges, he carried something I had never truly seen up close—a quiet, steady faith in God and a genuine love for Jesus. It wasn't loud. It wasn't performative. It wasn't wrapped in religion. It was simply who he was.

Without even realizing it, Mark would become the one who gently and subtly, led me to Jesus—not through pressure or preaching, but through the way he lived and loved. He was my safe place to explore and learn to walk in faith.

In God's perfect timing, nearly another year and a half later the chapter I had been waiting to close for years finally came to an end. My divorce was finalized. I didn't walk away angry. I didn't carry hatred with me. What I felt was relief, layered with a deep, complicated sadness—sadness for the situation, for the years that had led here, and for all the people who were touched by it.

I had hoped the ending could have looked different. I had hoped we could close that chapter with a kind of grace that few are fortunate enough to experience. But regardless the door was now shut.

On that very day, something rose up in my spirit with a clarity I couldn't ignore.

Jeremiah 29:11—"For I know the plans I have for you," declares the Lord, "plans to prosper you and not to harm you, plans to give you hope and a future."

Not sure where or how that verse came to land in my spirit. I wasn't active in church, studying the Bible, or living a Christ like life at that moment. I didn't understand why that verse was stirring in me, but I knew I needed to follow it. So, I did something I had never done before in my life:

I went out to Amazon searching… I bought a Bible—Not to hide in a drawer. Not to keep out of obligation. But to place openly in my home—on display—it would be a declaration of something new—A hope in the future.

It was the first Bible had ever purchased for myself. I didn't realize it then but it was the first step toward the God who had been pursuing me all along. That Bible became more than a book. It became a marker. A quiet beginning of a pursuit I didn't yet understand—but one God had already prepared.

That day wasn't just the ending of a legal marriage, it was a stepping stone toward my awakening. The beginning of setting me on the path to discovering who He truly was—and who I truly was in Him. The beginning of God rebuilding what had been broken for so long.

That single verse, that had been whispered into my spirit would become the framework for everything that God was silently working to unfold.

Change of Heart

Mark and I had both sworn we were done with marriage. We'd survived divorce, and that was enough for a lifetime. Or so we thought. God had other plans. Seven months after my divorce finalized, Mark and I stood together and made a covenant before God. It was the natural unfolding of something God had been weaving before either of us understood it.

This marriage felt different from the very beginning. This one was built on peace, steadiness, and a love that would reflect God's heart. It was ordained by God. "What God has joined together, let no man separate." (Matthew 19:6) For the first time in my life, I understood what that meant. This wasn't a union I created out of emptiness.

The was a union God Himself had coordinated by planting a vivid dream. That dream is what changed my heart toward marriage. In that dream there so much joy, peace, and love—I had felt completeness—I felt whole.

When we became engaged, the wedding was planned within a week replicating the dream that God had given me. The actual wedding, that's a fun story for another time. Most importantly, we were no longer living in sin but living as husband and wife.

I believed God was real, but I held my distance.

And yet, even with my hesitations, God began to bless us. He blessed us abundantly. I can only imagine those blessings came from the obedience in following Him with our marriage.

He rebuilt what the enemy had tried to destroy. He placed layers of protection around our home, our marriage, our finances, and our hearts. But where God moves, the enemy lurks. And he did.

He pounced with several back—to—back attacks—the kind that knock the wind out of you, the kind that make you question what next. By the time the last blow hit, I was growing anxious, exhausted, and overwhelmed. In the heaviness, there was a pull in my spirit—a quiet draw I couldn't ignore. Something in me whispered the answer wasn't to retreat, but to rise.

As a couple we had not been active in church. We visited a few times – usually on special occasions with his parents over the years but not consistently. One September Sunday morning, I had internally declared enough. I was going to church. Mark had undergone rotator cuff surgery from an accident in the midst of trying to build our home. I had no expectation he would go. I just knew I was going.

There is a kind of stillness that comes when you run out of strength. It does not feel spiritual. It's the flesh… it's tired—and I was tired.

I knew we were under an attack. He was coming to kill, steal, and destroy and we needed help. I needed help.

Freshly out of surgery just a few days prior with an arm brace and managing through the pain Mark surprisingly joined me. I walked into that church carrying years of confusion, layers of fear, and the weight of every attack.

I didn't know what I was looking for as I walked through the doors. I didn't even know what exactly what it was I believed—but I knew where I needed to go.

On that day—that ordinary Sunday—the beginning of a revelation would occur that would change everything. It was the day God began to water the seed in me that had been planted for decades. This would become the day my active pursuit of a relationship with my heavenly Father began.

Cracks

That day, the music began just like all the times before when we had visited over the years. Most songs were unfamiliar, words I had never memorized, melodies I had never heard. I would attempt in my tone-def voice to sing the words on the screen.

Something felt different this day. Something in me felt different. I was feeling desperate in all that we were enduring. I didn't know if God had an answer but I had enough belief to know I needed His help.

As they sang, the tears started building. Before I could stop it, they began to fall—silently, steadily. I couldn't understand what was happening—why was I crying. It was just a song. This was new. This was unexpected. Then in came the panic.

I'm crying. What are people going to think?

That thought hit me like a reflex learned from a lifetime of hiding my emotions. I had spent years keeping myself together, staying strong, staying quiet, staying composed. Tears were weakness. Tears were exposure. Tears were dangerous.

I had a total lack of understanding of what had just occurred. Something deep inside me had cracked. Something I had buried for decades. Something God had been waiting to touch. "I will give you a new heart and put a new spirit within you…" (Ezekiel 36:26) In that very moment it was just that. God's touch was softening a heart that had been hardened by fear, rejection, and survival. He was cracking the walls I had built and reinforced. He was reaching places I had hid away.

When the service ended, I walked out of that sanctuary feeling something… but I didn't understand what. I wasn't used to being undone or rattled. I wasn't used to feeling anything that deeply. I certainly wasn't use to publicly showing any sign of raw emotion. Something had been touched that I didn't even know was there. "Deep calls unto deep…" (Psalm 42:7) That's exactly what it felt like—God was calling to something deep within me.

When we returned home, I couldn't shake it. I replayed the morning church service, trying to relive the words that had caused my hardened shell to crack. "My sheep hear My voice, and I know them, and they follow Me." (John 10:27) I didn't recognize His voice yet, but something in me responded to it.

Using the words of the song, I searched online until I found the title of the song. Then out to Apple Music to purchase it. *Through the Fire* would be the first Christian song I would purchase.

Later that day, I sat with Mark and tried to put words to what had occurred at church, still puzzled and questioning the experience. *"I don't know why I was crying, I don't understand it"*, I told him. This moment became the beginning of something new between us—not just as husband and wife, but spiritually. It was the start of him becoming my sounding board, my safe place to process what I did not yet understand, the one who helped me make sense of the things God was beginning to stir in me.

He listened without judgment. He didn't dismiss it. He didn't over-spiritualize it. He simply said, with a calm certainty I didn't yet have, *"That was the Holy Spirit moving."* His words were slowly registering. The. Holy. Spirit. Moving—In. Me. Could that really be possible…

That feeling… the one that had wrapped itself around my heart and squeezed until the tears finally came—that was the Holy Spirit?

Something certainly got into me, but I was still apprehensive to the possibility. "The Spirit Himself testifies with our spirit..." (Romans 8:16) That day, the Holy Spirit spoke to my spirit through a song. That began a shift in me. But that was just the beginning.

I had simply been sitting there, very much aware of my need. But God touched the piece He needed first, my heart. I wasn't instantly changed. I wasn't suddenly washed clean in that moment, but something changed.

Surrender—asking Jesus to be my Lord and Savior—came later in that same service. I had done that quietly under the radar without a need to publicize it, not even to my husband.

I had finally reached for Him. God had been there all along, waiting. Patient. Unmoved by the years I had spent running in the opposite direction.

God had begun the first step of breaking away the layers I had spent a lifetime forging. Those walls had not been built overnight. They were formed slowly—layer by layer—through pain, disappointment, fear, and survival. Every hurt had become another brick. Every betrayal another layer of mortar. I had convinced myself those walls were necessary, that they were protecting me. In reality, they had been imprisoning me.

That song—unmistakable and undeniable—became the beginning of something I had never experienced before. It was more than music. It was an invitation. An initiation into a relationship with God that was no longer distant or theoretical, but deeply personal.

"Draw near to God, and He will draw near to you." (James 4:8) The instant I reached toward Him, He met me there.

All it took was one song to create the first crack in the walls I had spent years building to be unbreakable. What I thought had been reinforced with strength was actually fragile in the presence of His grace. That melody slipped past every defense I had constructed and reached a place in my heart I had long buried.

It was not loud. It was not dramatic. But it was undeniable.

The walls did not collapse instantly, but they had finally begun to crack. Through those cracks, the light of God's love would shine through.

And now—I WANTED MORE.

Hunger

That moment in church didn't just awaken something in me—it ignited
a hunger I couldn't ignore. A pull. A curiosity. A need to understand
the God who had touched me so deeply. I went back the next Sunday.
And the next. And the next. Before I even realized it, church had
become part of my weekly rhythm—not out of obligation, not out of
routine, but out of a longing I couldn't explain. Something in me
needed to be there. Something in me knew I needed God.

But with that hunger came questions—more questions than I
knew what to do with and in some cases, Mark too.

Who am I to worship God or Jesus?

How do you pray—and how do you do it "right"?

How do you know if God hears you?

How do you know if it's His voice or your own thoughts?

The questions came fast and furious, and instead of running from
them, I ran toward them. I spent daily time reading the Bible—
sometimes understanding, sometimes confused, but always searching. I
read books on prayer, on the Holy Spirit, on hearing God's voice, on
the basics of Christianity. A lot of the things that most people learn as
children, I was learning at forty-three.

I didn't just read—I cross-referenced everything with Scripture. I
needed beyond anything and everything—absolute truth. I needed
clarity and validation. I prayed daily for understanding of His Word.

Sundays consisted of being present in body for any moving of the
Holy Spirit during the service. Sunday evenings were reserved for

round two of the same service. This round would be a replay of the online streaming with my Bible, pens, and note pad ready. I wanted to fully understand the scripture and the message.

I wasn't going to build my faith on emotion alone. I needed to be anchored in the Word. "Your word is a lamp to my feet and a light to my path." (Psalm 119:105) Slowly, that lamp began lighting places in me I had kept hidden for years.

This relationship with God didn't come easy. It wasn't instant. It was far from effortless. I had to put the work in—the reading, the praying, the asking, the wrestling, the seeking, and the learning.

Even now, it continues to grow daily. Every question leads to another. Every revelation opens a new door. Every moment with Him uncovers something deeper.

But one of the hardest parts wasn't learning about God—it was learning to forgive myself for my own sins and the softening of my heart. Learning to die to the flesh daily, which included repeatedly giving my pain to God.

I had seen enough fake in my life. And in some areas, I had been fake myself—but never about my faith. That was a space I would not touch. Even during times when I was unsure, the fear of God kept it off limits.

My grandfather's judgment of my other grandfather as a hypocrite had left a mark. Those fears kept me guarded. Even when I didn't know much, I knew God did not tolerate anything falsely done in His name. That would forever be a line I would not cross. No thank you. The enemy already fought me enough. No way I would dare to risk the wrath of God too.

I struggled with showing my faith. Even though I was actively walking it out, I carried a deep fear of judgment and ridicule. I was afraid of standing publicly for something and failing privately.

What if people called me a hypocrite?
What if they questioned my sincerity?

Strangely enough, I could accept being called a sinner—that felt familiar. But the idea of being labeled a child of God terrified me. That title felt too holy, too weighty, and too exposed. I had never talked about my faith before. I didn't openly discuss God.

Why—because I simply didn't feel qualified. I knew all my flaws all too well. I knew how unpolished, untrained, and inexperienced I was. Everything about this new life felt foreign to me. In my mind, all of that disqualified me from opening my mouth.

Growing up around things I didn't understand—including the exposure to witchcraft, I was confused, cautious, and unsure of what was safe to speak about. I didn't want to be misunderstood. I didn't want to be judged. I didn't want to be associated with anything dark ever again. So, I stayed silent. Retreating back to what I knew. Not because I didn't believe—but because I didn't believe I belonged. I felt tainted.

I needed to be seen as strong, collected, polished even—that was safe. Being raw, vulnerable, imperfect—I was not comfortable with. My flaws, my wounds, my insecurities… I kept them buried, terrified they would be exposed for judgment by the holy ones surrounding me. I carried enough self—criticism to silence myself for a lifetime, I certainly didn't want anyone else's.

But God wasn't asking me to be perfect. He wasn't asking me to be polished. He wasn't asking me to perform. He was asking me to come—just as I was. Just as He had found me and awakened me.

Little by little, He began breaking the lie that I wasn't qualified. He would teach me that the very things I thought disqualified me had a purpose. This was the beginning of learning not just about God—but learning who I was to God. And that would change everything.

Safe Place

When I began this new journey—a path of understanding, healing, and learning who God truly was—there was so much I didn't yet know. I had misunderstood and misinterpreted quite a bit. There was so much I was beginning to see clearly for the first time. Clarity unfolded bit by bit and it was truly surreal.

In that season, where the Spirit pulled me, Mark became my encouragement. Where fear tried to silence me, he spoke life. Where doubt tried to cloud my vision, he reminded me of truth. And the places where I felt unsteady, he stood firm.

He didn't lead me by force or pressure. He simply walked beside me with a steadiness at my pace. He supported me as I learned to walk with God. He was my safe place.

A Living Sanctuary

I had never had a home secured or grounded in the protection that only God can provide. That spiritual fog I grew up in stayed with me, following me into every adult home environment I had stepped into. Those fogs were—heavy, dark, rooted in the enemy's presence.

I had learned demonic forces are always looking for a way in, always trying to penetrate. I knew I wanted peace, and home was going to have to be the place where that peace resided. If you don't have peace in your home, your spirit never finds rest or rejuvenation from the outside world. I wanted that safe and secure place with divine protection from the darkness outside.

We were living next door to the home we had been trying to build—the same home that had been met with challenge after challenge. That exact build which kickstarted my walk with God. Finally, the foundation was poured and the block was laid.

On February 28, 2024, in the middle of a workweek, a light drizzling day, my spirit stirred with something. I knew of evil's tactics and influence. This new home needed to be rooted in Christ. Covered by the blood of Jesus. And it was up to me to embed that covering— and it needed to be now. The next day they were bringing gravel for the concrete pad, so if I was going to do this, now was the time.

My home needed the spiritual protection that only God can provide. I locked my computer, stepped away from my work—from— home job, and went trudging through the damp muck. I carried the Bible I bought in 2022 when my divorce had finalized, and a permanent marker. Standing in what would be the center of my future home, I prayed silently, asking God to keep His hand wrapped around this space so that no evil would be permitted to enter. My future home was dedicated to be a sanctuary where God would be honored.

I took out my marker and wrote on the inside block foundation Matthew 7:25 "and the rain fell, and the floods came, and the winds blew and beat on that house, but it did not fall, because it had been founded on the rock."

When Mark came home, I told him—simply—that I had written scripture on the foundation. I was a little apprehensive about how he'd react. Something boldly faith related was outside my wheelhouse. This was a step I had taken in obedience. A step toward building the kind of home I had never known, but was determined to create.

Scripture

The dreary day when I prayed over my home was only the beginning. Once the concrete pad was poured, I returned that night with a permanent marker in hand and consecrated it. Along all four outer perimeters—where the walls would soon stand—I wrote scripture and the same prayer I had spoken before.

All throughout the build, scriptures speaking to God's divine love, protection, and peace were written on studs and walls. I wanted this home to be rooted in the Word from the ground up.

Every scripture I chose for our home I wanted to remember. I did something I had never done before—I highlighted them in my Bible with my trusty green highlighter. Until then, I had always treated a Bible as something too holy and sacred to mark in any way. I used to hold a strong belief writing in it was disrespectful, even desecrating.

Now, when I'm studying, sitting in a church service, or just casually reading, and I see that green highlighting—the color I reserved only for the scriptures that went into my home—my memory goes straight back to where each verse sits in my home. It also reminds me of the moment my Bible shifted from something I kept "untouched" to a personal resource I rely on daily.

Environment Matters

Our home was finally completed. The day after the walls were painted, I took a black metal cross from our temporary home, and had Mark to hang it above our front doors. That black metal against the bright white wall stood out immediately. It was bold, simple, and exactly where it needed to be. It was also the very first item ever to be hung in our home.

Today when you walk into my home, you'll see pieces of my faith throughout that was slowly intertwined. That cross at the entry. Another black metal piece of art—The Last Supper—hanging in my kitchen. A quote over my bed that reads, "Give it to God and Go to Sleep." My Bibles sitting next to my chair, not for display but because I actually use them. They stay there out of convenience for reading, studying, and cross-referencing. A bookcase filled with the Christian books I've read along the way.

None of it is staged. None of it is for show. These are the things I reach for, and the things that have helped me grow. These things remind me daily who I belong to and who has wrapped his love and protection over my life and our home.

This house was built with scripture in the foundation, covered in prayer during the framing, and finished with the things that keep my focus on God. The items on the walls and shelves aren't decorations— they're part of the environment I want and choose to live in. They're reminders of the journey, the protection, the peace, and the relationship that surrounds this home. Daily reminders when the flesh is weak, and no matter what life challenges come, I am held.

Allowed In

If you enter my home, you'll likely hear gospel music either coming
from my playlist or playing through Google Home stations. If the TV
is on, my choice is usually gospel music from YouTube with my
favorite channels, Son Life Broadcasting Network, or one of the many
pastors I follow.

All of this is done not because I'm suddenly some "holy" person
who has it all together. I'm not. I'm human, and fall short daily of the
glory of God. This is simply the environment I want and choose to
create—one that helps me learn and grow, but also one that sets the
tone of the atmosphere.

The presence of God is welcome here. The forces of darkness are
not. What you allow into your environment has a way of entering your
spirit. The things you watch and the things you listen to can be strategic
opportunities for darkness to penetrate. The enemy will use them as
tools to unsettle your spirit and pull your focus away from God. I've
lived long enough and have first-hand experience to that, so I'm
intentional about what fills the air in my home.

I've lived in places before where the air felt heavy, where
confusion and tension seemed to sit in the corners. Crystals, sage, and
candles were to be some form of protection against evil. I refuse to let
that be the case here. The music, the preaching, the worship in my
home—it's not just noise. It's part of the covering. It keeps my mind

focused, my spirit steady, and my home aligned with the One who protects it all.

This is my secure place. My reset. My reminder that God rebuilt my life from the inside out, and this home stands as proof of that rebuilding. What once felt broken, He patiently restored. A reflection of His grace and His mercy. This home is more than just a roof and walls—it is a testimony that God can rebuild a life stronger and better than it was ever was before.

Surrender

I had been actively seeking God because I knew I needed Him. I wanted more of Him. I already had a full plate with a full-time job, in the middle of building a home, and then an unexpected surgery but I made room for God. I went on a weekend retreat, hoping for clarity and peace.

When the first day came, the excitement I'd felt about this opportunity and experience now sat heavy on my chest. The weight of daily life responsibilities present but more than that condemnation hit me like never before.

Condemnation pressed in from every side. I questioned if I belonged there. I questioned if I had made a mistake. And underneath it all, I questioned what this weekend away from home would do to my home and my marriage. Let me be clear my marriage was solid, but the enemy planted an unfounded fear.

The enemy was using all his tricks attacking me with my fears and insecurities. Mark and I had been married only a couple of years, and since the day of our first date, we had never spent this type of time apart. Mark had driven me up, which meant I was stranded with no vehicle. I was—alone, in a foreign cabin, in the dark, with zero control over my environment. I was totally alone in that unfamiliar stillness with absolutely no distractions. Things I had buried and ran from I was forced to confront.

Crushing fear came rushing in.

Fear about my life. Fear about my marriage. Fear about my worth.
What if he realizes he enjoys life without me?
What if I'm not enough?

I lay there in the darkness, and the tears broke through. My heart breaking. It was the same emptiness that had followed me since childhood. In that moment—when I had nothing left to hold myself together—I knew I could not keep fighting this internal battle alone. Total surrender would be necessary.

God then spoke to the deepest part of me. Not in an audible voice, but in a knowing that pierced straight through the years of confusion,

"This is fear—of being abandoned. Fear of never being enough—deserving of love."

It was the first time in my life I understood the root of my pain. Once I could name it, I could finally begin to process it. "You will know the truth, and the truth will set you free." (John 8:32)

God didn't just reveal the wound. He revealed there was purpose behind the journey. He showed me how every moment—every disappointment, rejection, and spiritual battle—had led to the deep root of abandonment. Everything had led to this very moment of understanding and breakthrough.

My faith to trust Him would be my long-awaited release from this lifelong bondage I carried.

Deliverance doesn't begin with strength. It begins with surrender. That was the beginning of the healing that I needed. Not just from the pain—but from the lie and the anxiety that I had been alone in.

God was already preparing to rewrite the story the enemy had tried to narrate since my childhood. A narrative about love and a God who never abandoned me—even when I believed everyone else had. "The Lord Himself goes before you and will be with you…" (Deuteronomy 31:8)

Roots Exposed

Once God revealed the truth behind my fear, the real work began. Revelation is a gift—but healing is a process. For the first time in my life, I wasn't just reacting to the pain. I was finally able to see the root beneath it.

Fear had been the quiet narrator of my entire story. Fear had shaped my decisions. Fear had dictated my relationships. It had whispered lies into every corner of my identity. Now that the root was exposed, God began pulling it up—gently, but firmly.

Healing didn't come in a rush. It unfolded in layers — sacred moments of holy interruption where God met me exactly where I was and built my trust in Him. There were days I felt lighter, like something had finally lifted. There were days I felt raw, like a wound had been reopened. But in the discomfort, I could sense God doing something deep—something I had never allowed Him to do before.

He wasn't just healing the scars. He was healing the fears behind the scars. "Perfect love casts out fear…" (1 John 4:18)

I began to notice the patterns I had lived in for years: The bracing myself for rejection even when no one was rejecting me. The way I expected abandonment even in safe relationships. The way I apologized for existing, as if I were a burden. The way I clung to control because I didn't trust anyone.

These were survival mechanisms—the armor I had built as a child to protect myself from wounds. But God wasn't asking me to survive anymore. He was teaching me how to live. Living required letting Him into places I had kept locked down for decades.

It was uncomfortable. It was unfamiliar. But it was holy. Every time I surrendered a piece of the fear, He replaced it with truth. Every time I let go of a lie, He filled the empty space with His presence. Every time I loosened my grip on control, He showed me that I was never meant to carry the weight alone.

This was the beginning of deliverance—not the dramatic kind people talk about, but the quiet kind that rewrites a life from the inside out. God wasn't just healing what happened to me. He was healing what I believed because of it. For the first time, I felt hope where fear had lived for so long.

The Past

There was still a part of my story I had kept tucked away—the part I was afraid to say out loud. The parts that felt too dark, too confusing, too tangled with things I didn't fully understand.

For years, I carried the weight of what I had been exposed to in my childhood—the card readings, the spiritual atmosphere, the dreams and visions that felt too vivid to ignore. I just knew that it left a mark on me. A heaviness. A sense that something that had followed me into adulthood.

Even after I gave my life to God, that fear lingered in the background.

What if those experiences meant something was wrong with me?

What if the visions were evidence of something dark inside or attached to me?

What if God Himself rejected me because of where I came from?

I wrestled with those questions privately and silently—because the last thing I wanted was for someone to look at me and see darkness instead of deliverance.

Especially Mark.

He was steady. Gentle. He was my safe place. But even with him, I hesitated. I was uncertain how he would respond. I didn't want him to think I was crazy or unstable. And worst of all, I didn't want him to think I carried something demonic.

I held it in. I carried it alone. I tried to outrun the memories, the dreams, the spiritual confusion that had shaped so much of my childhood. But God has a way of bringing things into the light—not to shame us, but to free us. "There is no fear in love, but perfect love casts out fear." (1 John 4:18)

I finally shared that I had "experiences" spread throughout my life. I told of grandmother's card reading, the dreams, and visions. My heart raced. I braced myself for rejection and judgment. But instead, he listened. He didn't flinch. He didn't pull away. He didn't look at me like I was broken or dangerous.

I had not taken into consideration, it was a small town. He knew my family. He had already had known of the card reading I was raised around.

Yet, he still chose to loved me.

In that moment, something shifted. The darkness I feared wasn't in me—it was around me, from the environment I grew up in. I had confusion that stemmed from the lies I had believed. Speaking it out loud didn't expose me—it freed me for the first time.

That conversation with Mark became another turning point. Not because he had all the answers, but because he held space for my truth. Because he reminded me that God had been protecting me long before I ever understood.

It was during this time that God began showing me something I had never considered: the attacks over my life were not punishments from Him. They were not signs of His rejection. They were the enemy's continuous attempts to break me—and the very things that would later strengthen my faith.

Amazing Grace

The week before the women's retreat, during the Sunday worship
service, there was an altar call following a deeply touching sermon.
A mother and her two daughters—women who sing like angels, voices
that carry an unmistakable anointing—began to sing. It was beautiful,
I'm sure. But I couldn't hear them. The moment their voices lifted,
something shifted.

Their song faded, and in its place, I heard *Amazing Grace*—but
not the version I had known. This was the most peaceful, heavenly
melody I had ever encountered. The version I knew of this song did
there was no peace—only sorrow.

This song had been played at my brother's funeral in 2004, and
for twenty years it ripped open wounds. Emotions I absolutely did not
want to feel. If it came on the radio, I changed it instantly. I would not
let myself touch the pain it caused in my heart.

But this version was different. The melody wrapped around me
with hope and love. Peace. A gentleness I did not associate with *that*
song.

Mark physically sat beside me as the music played in my mind. As
clearly as if I were watching a TV scene unfold, I could see him
standing in front of me at the altar with his hands raised. The vision
only deepened the peace I felt. Mark had never left his seat. He was still
physically sitting next to me during this experience.

That afternoon at home, I was consumed with what I had felt. I
opened Apple Music and began searching for *that* version—the exact
melody I had heard in my spirit.

For over an hour, Mark listened to snippet after snippet from across the room as I searched. Finally, he asked, "What are you doing?" This was a moment of decision. I hesitated… but felt the need to tell him about my experience—of hearing this song earlier in church. I made that leap and waited for his reaction.

Instead of confusion or concern, he simply offered different artists to try. *That* reaction was totally was not what I had expected. I never found the exact version, but I found one close—and somehow, the pain that song once carried had begun to be replaced.

Later that night, lying in bed, I took another leap of faith. I told him about the vision part of my experience—seeing his hands raised during that song.

What I had no line of sight to was that there was a long—standing tradition he had once been part of where the men would sing *Amazing Grace* to their wives. I had never seen it or even heard of the tradition. Mark hadn't participated in years. In that moment of our conversation he hadn't thought that far in advance to even realize that was coming.

That following Saturday evening, to my complete surprise, my husband walked into the room with the other men—white shirts, red bow ties—and they began to sing *Amazing Grace*.

My mouth opened, but no words came. It was the exact melody I had searched for so desperately the week before. The moment when the men lifted their hands while singing, something inside me broke free.

The vision I had seen was unfolding right in front of me. This moment was drenched in love. Not sure if anyone else saw it but my husband had a heavenly glow and warmth radiating. My heart melted completely. That song was now fully imprinted only with love. The grief had been replaced.

At that moment, I knew. Even more than that—Mark knew—I wasn't crazy. My visions were not my imagination. My loving Father had known this moment was coming long before either of us had realized. He knew the deep pain I had which I refused to touch.

He lovingly replaced my pain—fully, completely—with peace and a beautiful memory. When I hear that song now, I look for my husband. I can't take my eyes off him. I wait eagerly for him to join in, almost holding my breath waiting for it. I look for that same glow of love I saw pouring out of him that night.

This became a confirmation—proof of the true source of my "experiences" were God given gifts. A glorious moment between Mark and I would have missed if I hadn't shared out loud the vision God had given me. We have a loving God who knows our needs even when we don't. With His mercy, He provides his children His *Amazing Grace*.

Obedience

I was afraid of public opinion and judgment. Along the way, I had absorbed the belief that faith and a relationship with God were supposed to be private. Anything public felt like performance, and I wanted no part of that. That was another lie, one that took time for me to recognize and even longer to overcome.

I didn't understand why people raised their hands in worship or why they shouted *"Amen"* and *"Hallelujah"* with such boldness. I certainly didn't understand falling out in the Spirit, running the aisles, or speaking in tongues. To me, it was all foreign, loud, and overwhelming. Yet watching people I respected—people whose personalities were normally calm and reserved—suddenly express *that kind of passion* became *intriguing.* It was so outside of their usual character that I couldn't ignore it.

I would find myself wondering what it must feel like to have that kind of emotion and devotion overflowing.

I was hesitant—I had a lot of questions.

It wasn't until I finally allowed myself to ask questions that things began to make sense. Mark explained it in a way that cut straight through my confusion.

"People will scream, shout, and lose their minds with passion at sporting events, races, and concerts—so why shouldn't we have that same passion for Jesus?"

Slowly… very slowly… I began trying to express that passion—
but only behind closed doors. In the privacy of my home, I would lift
my hands in praise as worship music played. It was an action I was too
afraid to show in public. But deliverance was coming.

There was a massive battle over my hands on my way to freedom.
I felt the pull and the anxiety wrestling inside me. The desire was there
to publicly display this kind of praise the way others so freely did. My
heart pounded through multiple Sunday services. My mind wrestled
with fear and condemnation that I wasn't worthy. Then one Sunday, I
finally surrendered. I lifted a single hand from my seat, feeling
completely exposed before everyone—and something broke.

It was a moment of freedom. Pure, holy freedom. Something so
natural for others felt like a massive leap for me. Like anything,
comfort comes with repetition. Now my hands eagerly lift in joy and
love towards my Father—both privately and publicly.

After lifting my hands in a worship service, the next hurdle I
would face was the altar call. I would feel the same pull—that
unmistakable draw of the Holy Spirit—but I stayed glued to my seat.
My mind raced with questions and insecurities:

*Me…at the altar? What will people think? Other people need prayer more
than I do. What am I supposed to do when someone prays for me? What if they ask
what I need prayer for?*

Those questions felt overwhelming, because the truth was… I
needed prayer for so much. I have been estranged from my children
since my divorce. My mother's heart aches every single day. I was
learning on the fly and trying to navigate a new journey with God that
felt both beautiful and terrifying. I carried wounds and fears I didn't
know how to release. I feared being seen, judged, and vulnerable in
front of people. All of this felt like exposure of my flaws and pain.

My spirit was being tugged forward, but fear kept me in my seat. I watched others walk to the altar with boldness I didn't yet have. I wondered if I would ever be brave enough to take that step.

One February Sunday morning, the service had stirred something deep in me. The Spirit was moving, and before I could talk myself out of it, I finally made my way to the altar.

Then—right as I got there—our pastor said something that made me want to crawl under the chairs.

He asked everyone to form two lines for a prayer line.

WAIT…WHAT…What did he say!
What the heck is that? I finally made it to the altar and now this!

I feel pretty safe saying I was the only one in the building who didn't know what it was. Quickly, I figured out what a prayer line was.

I thought I was going to be sick. My stomach flipped end over end. My knees felt weak. I honestly thought I might throw up. I wanted to crawl up under the chairs. All I could think about was how many people would be looking directly at me. But I took a deep breath and whispered in my heart:

Okay God… You got me up here. So here I go, trusting You.

I closed my eyes as the members began to lay hands on me, praying and speaking in tongues. I walked trembling, not daring to open my eyes. Part fear, part surrender—and somewhere in the middle of anxiety… a fire ignited.

I felt a touch that burned through my hands. In that moment I had assumed it was my blood pressure from the experience. I would very soon find it was not a physical heat, but a holy one—the kind that is a lifeline to the Father.

Two weeks after the prayer line, a significant purchase was made by my husband. My dear sweet, lovely husband called… *(yes, there is a bit of sarcasm there*) on a Thursday to tell me he had made a deal. I was excited for him up until he told me the price. The price was twice what we had originally discussed. I simply said, "Oh okay." I knew this was something we could use. More importantly he certainly deserved this. No way was I going to take his joy out of this moment.

We were in the middle of building a home. Internally, I was overwhelmed and unsure if this was the right financial move. The next morning was Friday. I knew I wanted—needed—God to be part of this already solidified decision. If nothing else, I just needed peace.

I lifted my hands for the first time in prayer. I asked Him to give me peace about this purchase and to protect us financially. I told Him that regardless of the outcome, I trusted Him and His will. As I sat there at my desk praying with my hands lifted in the air, they began to burn like fire.

I was terrified. I wondered if somehow that was God smacking my hands. *Had I done something wrong?* This was the first time I had ever prayed like this with my hands involved. I thought I was doing everything right. I had fervently asked for God to be part of this moment. I was sincerely submitting to His will. I didn't understand what was happening.

I finally caved and called my mother-in-law. I needed some spiritual guidance without judgment. I explained the purchase that was arranged and set to be picked up early the next week. I told her of my concerns with the purchase. I really focused on my experience in the prayer. I shared how my hands had burned. I questioned her if I had done something wrong.

I had associated fire at that time in my life, with evil—Hell, fire, and brimstone. She laughed tenderly and assured me that was not the case. She explained He had heard my prayer. As we continued to talk, I shared that same fire in my hands had occurred in the prayer line while others were speaking over me just a few weeks earlier. This was the start of my hands becoming my own prayer language with God.

Oh, and that purchase—the individual called the following Monday. The man we were buying from had a change of circumstances over the weekend and decided not to sell. Nothing short of divine intervention. God is good!

It took a lot of prayer and His repeated confirmation that He would provide for me before I could fully trust Him in this growing relationship. Even then, parts of me still trembled at the thought of anything public.

The conviction came to be baptized. It was late winter, and I tried to bargain with God. I'll do it when the church goes to the lake for baptisms. In my mind, that bought me time—time before I had to stand in front of everyone, time before I had to be seen.

In true fashion of our Lord, He holds us to the promises we whisper. Just a few weeks later, our pastor announced that a lake baptism was being planned. The lump in my throat hit instantly. I had made a promise, and now God was expecting me to follow through.

I talked to Mark about it, and of course he was supportive. But when June 30, 2024 arrived, the service itself was a blur. My mind was already at the lake, already wrestling with the anxiety of being watched. I felt like I was about to become a spectacle, and the weight of that sat heavy on my chest.

The drive to the lake was only a few miles, but it felt so drawn-out. When we arrived and I saw the crowd gathering, everything in me wanted to climb back into the truck and disappear. But I knew I had to honor my promise. When the pastors asked for a line, I was expecting to inconspicuously step into the back of the line. Nope, the next words out of his mouth, "shortest to tallest."

What… really? That puts me up front.

Taking a deep breath, I stepped into my place. I did it scared—but I did it. My pastors baptized me while Mark and his mom stood on the bank of the lake, witnessing that moment in my journey. I didn't know Mark had taken pictures until we got home. That night, I did something even more unthinkable for the old me: I posted those pictures on social media with the words:

Living in obedience with a public profession of my faith. Praise Jesus! Hallelujah!! Jeremiah 29:11–13

It took a lot of faith to publicly declare what I had felt. But I did it—trembling, terrified, and obedient.

And that obedience would become the doorway.

Another Spirit—led moment was still to come…

Long before I ever imagined myself doing anything publicly, I had a dream one night of our ladies' drama team performing… and there I was, right in the middle of it.

When I woke up, I actually laughed out loud. Not hardly, I thought. Not me. Not me up in front of everyone. I liked my quiet seat—the one safely tucked away where I could spectate, observe, and stay unnoticed.

But God knew. He knew the parts of me I was still hiding. He knew the gifts I didn't believe I had. He knew the fear that kept me small. He knew how to speak in a way I couldn't ignore. He has a way of nudging toward things I would have never considered or chosen for myself. And when I hesitated—and I did hesitate—He didn't back off. He just kept gently confirming it from different directions.

It was gentle, but it was clear: God was pushing me toward something that required more than silence, more than comfort, more than staying in the background. I was being called to step out.

The image from that dream kept resurfacing, so I began to pray. Eventually, I reached out to our ladies' drama lead and took yet another leap of faith. Everything in me felt unqualified and unworthy to stand beside those women. And the thought of being in front of everyone terrified me.

But I knew I was being led… so I did it anyway. I did it scared.

I practiced at home every single day with knots in my stomach so tight I thought they might choke me. And just when I didn't think it could possibly get any worse, the drama lead decided to switch things up. She split the team. Four to the stage. The rest stayed on the main floor.

Try to guess where she sent me.

Yep—*The stage.*

When she called my name and told me to head up there, I thought I might just fall out right there in the floor. Those four little steps felt like climbing straight up the side of a mountain. Once I got up there, it really felt like I was standing on top of that mountain. This mountain also included spotlights blazing down on me.

Inside, all I could say was, *"Really, Lord? Really?"*

The morning of my first performance, though, something shifted. I woke up and the fear wasn't there. No knots. Instead, there was this calm. A peace I couldn't explain if I tried. Joy that caught me off guard.

The best part of the experience, those ladies welcomed me with open arms. They didn't question my place. They didn't measure my worth. They simply embraced me.

Having never really had a tribe, for the first time, I felt like I belonged—like I finally fit somewhere. It was a small step in the natural, but a giant step in the Spirit.

Another door opened.

Another layer of fear peeled away.

Another reminder that obedience leads us into places we never imagined we could stand on our own.

In Progress

I am certainly not perfect. My life is far from perfect. Some relationships and areas of my life are not healed yet, and some may never be. There are places where I have had to hold boundaries with people I love—and that hurts. Some have chosen distance from me because of wounds I caused.

I continue to wait on God's timing instead of forcing my own. I have faith in a sovereign God—in His perfect timing and in His will— even when I don't understand it. He is working something for my good, even when I don't see it.

I pray for the people who have hurt me, but I also pray for the people I have hurt. Those who wounded me, I give forgiveness. Those I have wounded, I pray they can forgive me. More than anything, I continue to pray for the strength to forgive myself.

With continued obedience, I trust that God will keep touching the areas of my life that are still broken or unfinished. The progress He has already made in me has been life-changing, and I am forever grateful. I also know there is still more work to be done.

Obedience has now led me here—to writing this book and sharing elements of my testimony that I have never shared. Every chapter I write feels like another step of surrender. I know God can use the parts of my life I once tried to hide.

These pages are not the whole story—but they are a beginning. And for me, they are another massive leap of fait

Held

For decades, I thought I was marked by darkness. I was wrong. What tried to silence me did not succeed. What tried to confuse me did not win. What tried to haunt me never had the authority.

This chapter—and every chapter to come—isn't about the darkness I walked through. It's about the Light that found me and now leads me.

The lies have lost their power.

I am a woman held by God.

Restored.

Steady.

Certain of who I am and who I belong to.

Every moment I thought was breaking me was shaping me. Every place I felt abandoned, God was still holding me. Survival was never the end of my story.

I didn't earn my identity—I received it.

With the Holy Spirit flowing through me, I am not disqualified.

Not diminished.

Not defined by my past.

I have always been held.

"When you pass through the waters, I will be with you." (Isaiah 43:2)

This book is my YES to God's call for obedience—the scariest and boldest yet I have ever given. I am not sure where He will lead me next, but I am open and more prepared than ever to follow.

With newfound boldness and absolute sincerity, I say:

I trust where You lead.

Here I am, Lord.

Send me.

I know You have faithfully held me all along—And You always will.

You've made it through some of the hardest moments of my life with me in your reading of this book.

Maybe you're still sorting through your own story.

Just know this—God hasn't missed a single moment of it.

And He's not finished with either of us yet.

About the Author

Delphia Leffew is a Christian author and speaker whose life has been shaped by grief, trauma, and ultimately surrender. Through the loss of a child, years of silent endurance, and a long journey of healing, she discovered that what once felt like darkness was preparation for restoration, discernment, and purpose.

Her writing speaks to women who have learned to be strong but quietly feel exhausted—women who have carried grief, shame, abandonment, or spiritual fear in silence. With biblical clarity and lived experience, Delphia addresses spiritual warfare, identity, emotional healing, and the steady, layered process of transformation.

She is especially passionate about supporting women navigating pregnancy loss, child loss, relational strain, and seasons of rebuilding. Having walked through profound personal loss herself, she understands the isolation that often accompanies sorrow and the courage it takes to seek healing.

Delphia believes that healing is rarely instant, surrender is often quiet, and freedom is built through faithful obedience over time. Her message is simple: what once tried to haunt you can become the very place God holds you.

To connect with Delphia for speaking engagements or future resources:
Follow Delphia on TikTok: @delphia.leffew
Email: DelphiaLeffew@gmail.com

If this book encouraged you, consider leaving a review on Amazon to help other women find hope in their own journey.